Mastering Health Informatics: A Comprehensive Career Guide

Health informatics is reshaping the future of healthcare and the professionals who lead it. *Mastering Health Informatics* is the definitive guide for students, early-career professionals, and career changers who want to thrive in this high-impact, rapidly evolving field.

Written by a nationally recognized expert with over two decades of experience across federal health systems and higher education, this guide bridges the gap between classroom knowledge and real-world application. Whether you're exploring your first role or planning your next career move, you'll gain the insights, tools, and strategies needed to navigate the informatics workforce with clarity and confidence.

Inside, you'll find:

- Clear explanations of key competencies, tools, and certifications
- Career pathways from entry-level to leadership
- Case studies, job market insights, and salary trends
- Practical advice on resumes, interviews, and networking
- Resources for lifelong learning, advancement, and professional development

With a focus on digital health innovation, workforce readiness, and patient-centered care, this guide prepares you to make a meaningful impact at the intersection of healthcare, technology, and information science.

Empowering, accessible, and deeply informed, *Mastering Health Informatics* is more than a career guide, it's your roadmap to leading the transformation of healthcare through data and innovation.

HIMSS Book Series

Engage!
Transforming Healthcare Through Digital Patient Engagement, 1st Edition
Edited By Jan Oldenburg, Dave Chase, Kate T. Christensen, Brad Tritle

AI in Health
A Leader's Guide to Winning in the New Age of Intelligent Health Systems, 1st Edition
By Tom Lawry

Voice Technology in Healthcare
Leveraging Voice to Enhance Patient and Provider Experiences, 1st Edition
By David Metcalf, Teri Fisher, Sandhya Pruthi, Harry P. Pappas

Building Connected Communities of Care
The Playbook For Streamlining Effective Coordination Between Medical And Community-Based Organizations, 1st Edition
Edited By Keith Kosel, Steve Miff

mHealth
From Smartphones to Smart Systems, 1st Edition
Edited By Rick Krohn, David Metcalf

Clinical Surveillance
The Actionable Benefits of Objective Medical Device Data for Critical Decision-Making, 1st Edition
By John R. Zaleski

Beyond HER
Using Technology to Meet Growing Demands and Deliver Better Patient Care, *1st Edition*
By Jeffery P. Daigrepont, EFPM, CAPPM

The Digital Reconstruction of Healthcare
Transitioning from Brick and Mortar to Virtual Care, 1st Edition
By Paul Cerrato, John Halamka

The Handbook of Continuing Professional Development for the Health Informatics Professional, 1st Edition
Edited By JoAnn Klinedinst

The CPHIMS Review Guide, 4th Edition
Preparing for Success in Healthcare Information and Management System, 4th Edition
By Healthcare Information & Management Systems Society (HIMSS), Mara Daiker

Understanding Healthcare Cybersecurity, AI, and Emerging Technologies
Protecting Patients and Their Data
By Lee Kim

Mastering Health Informatics: A Comprehensive Career Guide
Unlocking Careers, Advancing Systems, and Transforming Patient Care through Information Science
By Christopher K. Gransberry, PhD

Mastering Health Informatics: A Comprehensive Career Guide

Unlocking Careers, Advancing Systems, and Transforming Patient Care through Information Science

Christopher K. Gransberry, PhD

Routledge
Taylor & Francis Group
A PRODUCTIVITY PRESS BOOK

Designed cover image: Shutterstock

First published 2026
by Routledge
605 Third Avenue, New York, NY 10158

and by Routledge
4 Park Square, Milton Park, Abingdon, Oxon, OX14 4RN

Routledge is an imprint of the Taylor & Francis Group, an informa business

ISBN: 978-1-041-17468-4 (hbk)
ISBN: 978-1-041-17466-0 (pbk)
ISBN: 978-1-003-68984-3 (ebk)

DOI: 10.4324/9781003689843

Typeset in Garamond
by SPi Technologies India Pvt Ltd (Straive)

To my loving children: Chris Jr., Trumaine, and Hayden. Your strength, curiosity, and laughter inspire me daily.

To my steadfast friends and supporters, thank you for reminding me to keep going.

To my students, past and present, may you always lead with purpose and never stop learning.

Contents

Preface

When I began my career in health informatics, I was driven by the vision of a more connected, intelligent, and patient-centered healthcare system, one where information science could bridge gaps, reduce errors, and empower decision-making. At the time, the field was still evolving. Electronic health records were gaining traction, but many institutions struggled with fragmented systems, staff resistance, and unclear data governance. Even then, I recognized that behind the technology were people, students, clinicians, analysts, and leaders trying to navigate a rapidly changing landscape with very little practical guidance.

That's why I wrote this book.

Mastering Health Informatics is a product of my journey as a professor, federal health IT executive, and lifelong advocate for the responsible use of technology in healthcare. It was born out of the countless conversations I've had with students seeking direction, with professionals transitioning into informatics, and with leaders trying to future-proof their organizations. This book exists to help you not just understand the "what" of health informatics, but the "how" and "why" and how to break into the field, why certain skills matter, and how to grow into a leader who makes a lasting impact.

The healthcare industry is experiencing an unprecedented digital transformation. Telehealth, artificial intelligence, interoperability standards like FHIR, and data-driven care models are reshaping every aspect of how we treat patients and improve outcomes. At the center of all this innovation is health informatics. It is no longer a support function; it is a strategic cornerstone of modern medicine. Informatics professionals are the translators, the bridge builders, the system designers, and the stewards of digital health equity.

This book serves as a guide for anyone, from students to seasoned professionals, who wants to unlock the power of information to advance healthcare. It is both a map and a compass: it outlines core competencies, explores career paths, examines real-world trends, and provides practical tools for success in a field that is as dynamic as it is impactful.

Whether you are exploring health informatics for the first time or looking to level up your career, I hope this guide offers clarity, inspiration, and tangible value. The future of healthcare depends on people like you, skilled, motivated, and ready to lead with both insight and integrity.

Welcome to the future of healthcare. Let's build it together.

-Christopher K. Gransberry, PhD

About the Author

Christopher K. Gransberry, PhD is a nationally recognized expert in health informatics, healthcare administration, and organizational leadership. With over two decades of experience spanning academia, federal health systems, and workforce development, Dr. Gransberry brings an unmatched depth of insight into the evolving world of digital health and information science.

He holds multiple graduate-level degrees and certifications across health informatics, healthcare operations management, organizational leadership, management information systems, and new business ventures. This diverse and rigorous academic foundation has fueled a career at the intersection of healthcare innovation, strategic planning, and systems transformation.

Professionally, Dr. Gransberry has led major programs and change initiatives in one of the largest integrated healthcare systems in the United States, contributing to national efforts in electronic health record modernization, benefits management systems, and data-driven policy implementation. His government service includes leadership roles in health informatics, project and program management, and change management, where he has influenced national strategies that shape the benefits delivery experience for millions of Americans.

As an educator, Dr. Gransberry has taught and developed dozens of courses across the fields of health information management, informatics, data analytics, and healthcare leadership. His students range from undergraduate learners to graduate professionals across health, business, and technology disciplines. Known for integrating real-world application with academic rigor, he is widely respected for his mentorship and commitment to student success.

Dr. Gransberry's research contributions include peer-reviewed publications on digital equity, instructional design, federal employee engagement, and leadership in public service. His work reflects a commitment to bridging theory and practice, with a focus on improving access, performance, and health outcomes through information systems.

Through this guide, Dr. Gransberry empowers readers to navigate the complex and exciting world of health informatics with clarity, purpose, and confidence. His voice, grounded in lived experience and scholarly expertise, offers aspiring professionals a practical, insightful, and inspiring roadmap to success.

Acknowledgments

Writing *Mastering Health Informatics: A Comprehensive Career Guide* has been a deeply personal and professionally rewarding experience. It would not have been possible without the individuals and institutions that have contributed to my growth and perspective along the way.

I would like to extend my sincere gratitude to the US Department of Veterans Affairs (VA), particularly the Veterans Benefits Administration, the Office of Health Informatics, and the national Health Information Management Program Office for the incredible opportunities, insights, and real-world experience that have shaped my understanding of digital health in service to those who have served our nation. The VA has been more than an employer; it has been a classroom, a proving ground, and a source of ongoing inspiration.

To my academic foundations, I am deeply grateful to the Master's in Health Informatics program at Louisiana Tech University and the Post-Master's program in Healthcare Operations Management at Nebraska Methodist College. These programs challenged and equipped me with the analytical, operational, and leadership skills needed to navigate and help shape the evolving landscape of health informatics.

To the many students I have taught and mentored over the years, your curiosity, ambition, and commitment to change have fueled my desire to write this book. Each question you asked, each project you pursued, and each success you achieved reminded me why this field matters. You are the future of health informatics, and I am honored to have been part of your journey.

This book is a reflection of the experiences we've shared and the progress we've made, together.

-Christopher K. Gransberry, PhD

Chapter 1

Introduction to Health Informatics

Welcome to the transformative and innovative guide to Health Informatics, a field where technology meets healthcare to create better patient prospects and enhance accessibility in all disciplines. From foundational and basic-level knowledge to advanced career goals, the book takes you through the journey step-by-step while maintaining your interest in growing evolution in this field. As the healthcare sector continues to innovate in the digital era, the opportunities to grow in different aspects are endless, which would inspire you to lead the way in this field. With dedication, motivation, and infinite courage, you have the power to change and drive the future!

Understanding Health Informatics: Definitions and Distinctions

The fast-evolving field of health informatics integrates data analytics and information technology with healthcare to improve patient results, administrative performance, and

DOI: 10.4324/9781003689843-1

community health accomplishments. Health informatics functions as the core system for medical data storage by allowing access and utilization for healthcare provider collaboration and individual patient care enhancement. The distinction between health information management (HIM) and health informatics stems from incorporating advanced technology to clarify clinical practices and simplify medical care procedures (Alotaibi & Federico, 2017).

The vital functions of health information processing depend on health information technology (HIT), which offers essential elements such as electronic health records (EHRs) and specialized hardware and software (Collen & Ball, 2015; Kaplan, 2020). Health Information Technology is a fundamental health informatics section that does not define the entire discipline. Health informatics extends past HIT technology because it contains essential theoretical and analytical systems for advancing fundamental healthcare transformations.

Bioinformatics is continually mistaken for health informatics, yet both entities possess separate focus points. Health informatics processes biological data specifically through bioinformatics and simultaneously bridges its operations across clinical operations, public health, and administrative entities. Technology enables health informatics practitioners to produce superior healthcare outcomes by analyzing medical data, which connects social health indicators with individual conduct and therapy information (Holzinger, 2016). Health informatics is a forceful interdisciplinary instrument to drive healthcare progression, thus allowing experts to construct unanticipated possibilities for future medical practice. Health informatics embraces public health informatics (PHI) as one of its subfields that applies informatics principles to enhance population wellness by focusing on surveillance and preparedness alongside prevention measures instead of direct treatment. The main objective of PHI is to operate in governmental departments alongside public sectors to decrease risks while stopping disease outbreaks by implementing time-sensitive data-based interventions (Aziz, 2017).

The Historical Arc of Health Informatics

The history of health informatics started in the mid-20th century, yet its contemporary format developed after healthcare systems adopted electronic record systems and increased computing capabilities. Diagnostic information received one of its first standardized capturing methods through the introduction of the International Classification of Diseases (ICD). In the 1970s, hospitals and academic organizations started testing the implementation of digital patient databases alongside clinical determination aid systems. The field experienced its first widespread implementation phase during the 2000s period.

A significant set of U.S. policy measures acted as driving forces that accelerated Health Informatics development throughout the nation. The Health Information Technology for Economic and Clinical Health (HITECH) Act of 2009 established the Meaningful Use (MU) program to encourage healthcare providers to use EHRs. The federal program generated technological adoption while requiring operational connections between systems and patient engagement and performance-based data analysis, according to Brewer et al. (2020).

Electronic record adoption established a whole new system that transformed healthcare operations. Health systems gained better care coordination abilities because a centralized database allowed them to track major disease patterns and identify patient trends through effective search capabilities. Public health agencies implemented real-time surveillance systems that helped prevent disease spread and control its transmission, particularly during emergencies and bioterrorism situations (Aziz, 2017).

The healthcare journey for patients worldwide has become more interactive due to the increased availability of internet-connected devices. The rise of patient portals accompanied by telehealth and mobile applications provided people with independent platforms to handle appointment scheduling, medication administration, and health data assessment.

Health Informatics as a Multidisciplinary Field

Multiple systems of analysis unite in health informatics because they incorporate information technology with clinical practice, behavioral science, statistics, and policy developments (M. O. Kim et al., 2017; Wachter, 2016). The projected success depends on multiple parties working together since each stakeholder offers different views and professional areas. The combination of clinicians delivering clinical delivery knowledge with IT professionals constructing the technology infrastructure represents successful collaboration to ensure data flow security.

Informatics progresses through artificial intelligence (AI) and machine learning (ML) integration because it demands multilateral team effort. Digital tools need thorough adjustment combined with input from clinical staff members, engineering professionals, and experts in data science. Research shows that healthcare professionals must guide the learning process through interactive machine learning (iML) because healthcare decision-making processes are ethically complex (Holzinger, 2016). The combined efforts between different specialists lead to enhanced algorithm performance and the assurance of dependable clinical interpretations.

Expert policy-makers and regulatory professionals have essential responsibility in this field. Medicine professionals create data governance systems to address security, privacy, and ethical challenges. The NHS's WannaCry ransomware attack emphasized the requirement for stringent cybersecurity policies, as shown in the study by Sheikh et al. (2021).

A successful health informatics system operates as a symphonic orchestra where different entities normalize their operations to enhance treatment quality and safety while maximizing productivity. Health services now require clinical information officers (CCIO) and digital health strategy roles because they combine medical intuition with technological expertise (Sheikh et al., 2021). Table 1.1 outlines foundational distinctions and components of the health informatics landscape. It helps clarify how this interdisciplinary field differs

Table 1.1 Key Concepts and Components of Health Informatics

Term/Domain	*Definition*	*Focus Area*	*Key Tools/ Functions*
Health Informatics	Application of IT and data analytics in healthcare	Patient care, clinical systems, decision - making	EHRs, CDSS, interoperability, analytics
Health Information Management (HIM)	Management of health records and coding standards	Documentation, compliance, coding	ICD-10, CPT, ROI, record integrity
Health Information Technology (HIT)	Tech systems enabling health data exchange	Infrastructure and software systems	EHR platforms, servers, cybersecurity tools
Bioinformatics	Application of informatics to molecular biology	Genomics, proteomics, research data	DNA sequencing tools, molecular databases
Public Health Informatics (PHI)	Informatics applied to population health	Disease surveillance, outbreak response	Dashboards, syndromic surveillance, GIS

from related domains and what core technologies and functions define its scope.

Emerging Trends and Innovations in Health Informatics

The quick transformation of health informatics occurs because of ongoing technological breakthroughs (Andreu-Perez et al., 2015; Veinot et al., 2018). Artificial intelligence systems that perform deep learning now handle challenging diagnostic operations, including examining radiology images and forecasting patient health conditions from electronic medical record information (Ravì et al., 2017). The benefits of these tools exist with great promise, though they need careful and deliberate application. Training data bias problems demonstrate their ability to sustain inequalities during various analyses of wearable health trackers and algorithmic triage systems (Brewer et al., 2020).

Healthcare interoperability is a dual purpose between transformational objectives yet extensive technical difficulty. Health data interoperability between different healthcare systems and institutions serves to preserve quality care and maximize the value of available information. The U.S. Interoperability and Patient Access Rule and eHealth exchange standards from Europe seek to create data connectivity by dismantling information barriers (Sheikh et al., 2021).

Healthcare transformation occurs when providers use patient engagement devices such as mobile health applications, wearable devices, and remote monitoring solutions. Health technology platforms enable patient autonomy in managing health problems and observing fitness targets and clinical interactions. The advancement of digital inclusion must be maintained at all times. Internet access coupled with low digital literacy causes communities to lag behind technological advancements, thus widening pre-existing health disparity gaps (Brewer et al., 2020).

Public health informatics develops new features by adopting tools, including geospatial mapping, syndromic surveillance, and real-time dashboards (Henry et al., 2016; Panayides et al., 2020; Xu et al., 2021). The tools that have been created enable quick health department responses alongside policymaker reactions to emerging infectious disease threats and natural disasters. The resource allocation strategies developed for crisis containment depend on the information collected by health information exchanges (HIEs) and public health information networks (PHINs) (Aziz, 2017).

Why This Book Matters

The discipline of health informatics is an essential force that helps healthcare organizations improve their care quality while establishing fair treatment and handling complex medical problems. The rising need for data-intensive healthcare produces value in using health information across different system levels through effective harnessing and analytics.

Your knowledge of fundamental health informatics principles and current industry trends will serve you well when entering this active profession as a student, clinician, or career changer. Figure 1.1 illustrates how the components of health informatics intersect and support the broader goals of healthcare innovation, patient empowerment, and data-driven practice. The book presents an educational guide that explains essential terms and displays employment opportunities to show healthcare informatics as an active, transforming discipline that effectively enhances patient care.

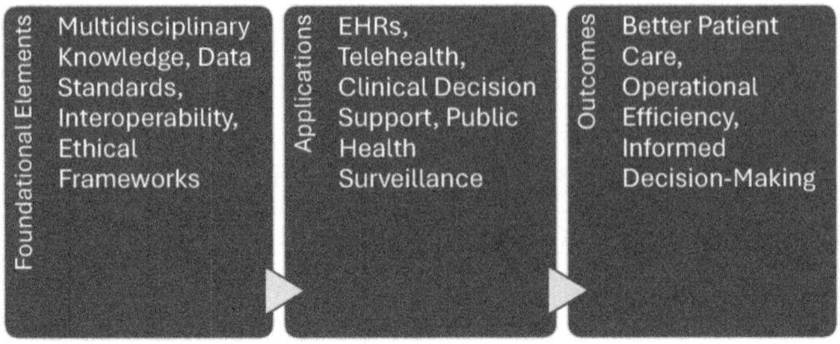

Figure 1.1 Foundations of Health Informatics.

This text unites practical components that enable you to handle your health informatics occupation with assured direction. The concepts in these chapters become our baseline understanding because they will guide system development, healthcare decisions, and patient care in the digital era.

Chapter 2

Core Competencies and Skills

After reviewing the background of health informatics, you would be keen to learn the core skills and traits for building a foundation in health informatics. This chapter will take you through different aspects such as competency domains, tools of the trade (SQL to FHIR), and various other technological aspects to familiarize you with the core dynamics of the field. This information will enable you to develop a basic foundation for strengthening the educational pathways and the career as we move through different chapters in this book.

Building the Foundation for a Future in Health Informatics

Health informatics is not just a field, it's a dynamic and transformative discipline that offers limitless potential for those ready to lead the future of healthcare. Your success in health informatics depends on mastering the fundamental abilities that describe successful professionals in this field. This

DOI: 10.4324/9781003689843-2

chapter reveals the vital technical capabilities and soft competencies employers want today, with descriptions of main software tools and evidence that communication and project management require absolute mastery.

In health informatics, you're not just working with data, you're empowering the future of healthcare by protecting sensitive information and fostering relationships that bridge different sectors. These competencies act as foundational elements to produce meaningful work that brings positive patient results and optimized medical workflows and maintains ethical technology standards in healthcare delivery. Your expertise in data sciences and informatics in healthcare will pave the way for innovative development to ensure healthcare quality. Figure 2.1 visually represents how a layered competency approach from foundational analytics to advanced leadership forms the basis of professional success in health informatics.

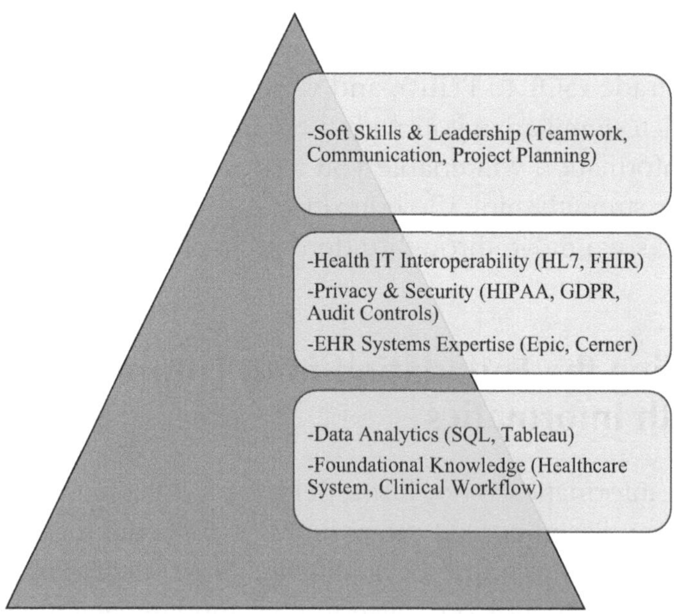

Figure 2.1 Building Blocks for Health Informatics.

The Competency Domains of Modern Health Informatics

Health informatics professionals need competencies including data analytics competence, EHR systems expertise, privacy and security awareness, leadership qualifications, and interpersonal communication capabilities (Chung & Zeng, 2017; Fernández-Luque & Bau, 2015). Each domain encompasses knowledge areas and capabilities necessary for the practical application of informatics in clinical, public health, and administrative settings.

The central core of many informatics roles exists within the data analytics domain. Healthcare professionals need abilities to organize and interpret standard and nonstandard medical information. Analytics core competencies today encompass three key competencies for health data analytics, which include data visualization, trend interpretation, and statistical reasoning, according to Monkman et al. (2023). The knowledge base of healthcare professionals should consist of data warehousing systems and population health tools to execute predictive modeling and risk stratification functions.

The competencies related to electronic health record systems include knowing how clinical data enters the system and how it is organized and accessed for integrated workflow use. Hospital-based positions and health systems require candidate experience with Epic and Cerner programming systems. Georgetown University researchers Sapci and Sapci (2020b) determined that students understand EHR concepts but still need valuable experience with practical healthcare technologies.

The protection of patient data falls under privacy and security competencies, which adhere to HIPAA, GDPR, and other relevant regulations. Data stewardship requires a basic understanding of role-based access control and encryption standards and security audit capabilities, according to

Table 2.1 Core Competency Domains and Associated Tools in Health Informatics

Competency Domain	*Key Skills/Abilities*	*Associated Tools/ Technologies*	*Example Applications*
Data Analytics	Data visualization, trend interpretation, statistical reasoning	Tableau, Power BI, Excel (Pivot Tables), SQL	Building dashboards, population health reports, predictive modeling
Electronic Health Records (EHR)	Workflow navigation, data structuring, EHR template customization	Epic, Cerner	Clinical reporting, patient data retrieval, system interface design
Privacy and Security	HIPAA compliance, encryption, audit controls, role-based access	Security Audit Tools, EHR Audit Logs	Data breach prevention, internal risk audits, role assignment in EHR
Leadership and Organizational	Systems thinking, strategic planning, budgeting, team coordination	Project Management Tools, Agile, Lean Six Sigma	Leading implementations, change management, team supervision
Health IT Interoperability	System integration, API use, message formatting	HL7, FHIR, SMART on FHIR	Health app development, cross-system communication, mHealth implementation
Interpersonal and Soft Skills	Communication, teamwork, cultural competency, stakeholder engagement	Collaboration Platforms (MS Teams, Zoom)	Bridging clinical and technical teams, cross-functional project collaboration

Garde et al. (2006). Modern healthcare security needs heightened attention because hospital networks face continuous ransomware attacks (Monkman et al., 2023).

People who want to steer projects and institutions and lead teams require leadership and organizational behavior competencies. According to Hsu et al. (2012), public health informatics professionals at middle-tier levels require leadership capabilities and systems thinking abilities to unite different departments and make informatics initiatives support organizational objectives. Educational programs for health informatics emphasize budgeting practices in addition to managerial planning and moral leadership during technical deployments. Table 2.1 offers a concise comparison of the core health informatics domains, highlighting the tools and real-world applications that define each area.

Tools of the Trade: From SQL to FHIR

The health informatics domain has introduced many new tools throughout the previous ten years. Public health informatics professionals must interact with expanding software programs, programming languages, and standard interoperability protocols.

Epic and Cerner are the leading electronic health record vendors whose products have expanded nationwide and internationally. Medical professionals who plan to work in clinical informatics must learn to use EHR interfaces, create clinical reports, and modify templates. According to Sapci and Sapci (2020a), most graduates cannot adapt to working with actual EHR systems unless their program provides deep training in such systems.

The market leaders in tools for creating visual analytics include Tableau and Power BI. The tools allow experts to design dashboards that reveal the transformation of complicated datasets into actionable narratives for stakeholders to execute decisions. The market selects job candidates who demonstrate competency with such tools, according to Sapci and Sapci (2020a).

Relational database querying requires using the Structured Query Language (SQL) as an essential requirement. The tool provides health professionals with precise methods to access and handle critical medical data. A basic comprehension of SQL provides substantial advantages for informatics professionals even if complete programming knowledge is unnecessary for their roles (Garde et al., 2006).

The exchange of health IT data depends on the essential components of HL7 alongside FHIR (Fast Healthcare Interoperability Resources). The healthcare industry uses HL7 as its traditional message formatting system, and FHIR delivers contemporary API-based solutions for mobile health applications and patient app connectivity (Monkman et al., 2023). Knowledge about these standards must be fundamental for workers in system integration and app development functions.

Soft Skills That Make a Difference

The practice of health informatics extends beyond technology because it focuses on relationships among people alongside processes and impact assessment. The same importance exists between having strong technical abilities and demonstrating fundamental leadership competencies, which include working with different domains, closing communication divides, and managing the overall project completion from start to finish.

The critical requirement in settings that combine IT specialists with clinicians, administrators, and policy-makers lies in team collaboration. According to Hsu et al. (2012), public health practitioners identified interprofessional collaboration as one of their most required competencies.

The implementation demands cultural adaptability from personnel alongside a shared dedication to patient-focused results.

Modern-day organizations do not restrict project management expertise only to executive positions. Modern informaticians are important leaders during EHR implementations, software rollouts, and workflow redesign initiatives. Health informatics professionals must build their proficiency in project planning and budgeting activities along with stakeholder engagement techniques, according to Kokol et al. (2018). Professional success in this field comes from working knowledge of Agile or Lean Six Sigma framework principles.

A Self-Assessment: Do You Have These Skills?

Readers are now asked to evaluate their abilities before recognizing their development needs. Below is a short assessment tool for your evaluation.

- The generation of descriptive statistics through pivot tables in Excel makes you feel comfortable with your operational skills.
- When talking to a stakeholder who lacks technical expertise about HL7 and FHIR, would it be possible for you to describe the differences between these systems?
- You have worked with people from other fields to fulfill shared project needs.
- Your readiness to guide a team toward successful project timeline completion is a vital requirement.
- Please outline the data privacy rules that affect digital health applications.

The book supports developing these competencies even if you answered any of the questions with doubts. Health informatics maintains a continuous learning process that requires students to progress as much as they strengthen their skills.

Summary and Reflective Prompt

According to this chapter, each health informatics professional must build these essential competencies as their fundamental educational foundation. All future healthcare contributors must master the required technical skills such as analytics, security, interoperability, and crucial social abilities such as leadership and collaboration to build meaningful contributions.

The concepts were supplemented with essential tools, which include Epic, Tableau, SQL, HL7, and FHIR, which help execute informatics in practice. The assessment tool helped you start your personal development progress when you learned about it toward the end of the course. Professionals must examine their current abilities and specify what knowledge and skills they intend to enhance throughout the following six months.

Chapter 3

Educational Pathways

After reading two chapters, the book might have taken you deep into Health Informatics, and you might be keen to pursue education in it. The educational pathways in this field are diverse and innovative, aligning with modern digital healthcare requirements. This chapter will take you through different prospects of pursuing education in this field, from very basic to the higher levels. The world of health informatics is waiting for passionate, driven individuals to lead the way, innovate, and make a real difference in patients.

Fundamental Steps to Obtain Health Informatics Education

Deciding on the correct educational pathway in health informatics is crucial for individuals interested in building or progressing their careers in this active field. Students at any stage of their academic careers, professionals seeking career changes, and international learners need a clear understanding of the available education paths. This chapter establishes an accessible motivational guidance system for explaining how

DOI: 10.4324/9781003689843-3

students should choose between different degree programs, accreditation standards, certification programs, and educational formats. The process will teach you to match your goals with the most appropriate educational plan and show you which credentials might help you get specific career openings.

Comparing Bachelor's, Master's, and Doctorate Programs

Multiple educational options exist in health informatics that follow specific academic levels that satisfy various learner profiles and diverse career objectives (Orji & Moffatt, 2018; Wilson & Maeder, 2015). Introductory college courses welcome new high school graduates and individuals who want to change their professional direction. The duration of such educational programs ranges between three to four years and includes essential coursework in anatomy, physiology, healthcare systems, computer science, and information systems. The later sections of the curriculum introduce specific health informatics subjects that cover data management, clinical decision support, and EHR systems (Bichel-Findlay et al., 2023a).

Graduates who earn bachelor's degrees in health informatics or related subjects qualify to take positions as data analysts, health information technicians, and IT support specialists within healthcare facilities. The curriculum of these educational programs focuses on broad knowledge that enables students to join forces for clinical, administrative, and technological health work (Kampov-Polevoi & Hemminger, 2011). Bachelor's graduates learn sufficient subject matter to become operational within healthcare but need specialized education to gain leadership authority.

Master's levels of study provide focused education, specializing in students in particular fields. These specialized programs direct their education to one to two years of training that builds health informatics expertise for healthcare workers, IT specialists, and business professionals. The curriculum offers more expansive lessons, including clinical data analytics, HL7 and FHIR interoperability standards, project management techniques, and HIPAA privacy regulations (Mantas et al., 2010). Capstone projects and internships are practical requirements that require students to use their theoretical informatics knowledge to address authentic challenges.

The PhD in biomedical and health informatics serves individuals who wish to work in academic and policy departments or hold executive-level positions. The study demands extensive learning in research methods and data science, machine learning knowledge, and ethical principles. The primary responsibility of doctoral students involves adding novel discoveries to the discipline through their original research activities (Hersh et al., 2022). Their efforts guide future standards development, and they contribute advice for healthcare technology development processes that guide public healthcare policies and medical procedures.

Each educational level extends the previous level by adding more sophisticated knowledge, greater professional accountability, and scope of impact. Master's and doctoral degrees allow students to pursue specialized knowledge and acquire leadership skills besides the information they learn in bachelor's degree programs. Table 3.1 provides a comparative overview of educational levels in Health Informatics, highlighting key features, career opportunities, and curriculum focus at each academic stage.

Table 3.1 Comparison of Health Informatics Educational Levels

Educational Level	*Duration and Entry Requirements*	*Key Curriculum Focus*	*Career Opportunities*
Bachelor's Degree	3–4 years; High school diploma or equivalent	Foundational health sciences, intro to informatics, EHRs, data management	Health data analyst, EHR technician, IT support in healthcare
Master's Degree	1–2 years; Bachelor's degree in health, IT, or business	Advanced data analytics, project management, HL7/FHIR, privacy laws	Clinical informatics specialist, project manager, interoperability analyst
Doctorate (PhD)	3–6 years; Master's degree recommended or required	Original research, policy, machine learning, ethics, leadership	Academic faculty, policy advisor, senior informatics executive

Understanding CAHIIM Accreditation and Its Significance

Students should use accreditation as their central quality assessment factor to select the right program. The United States uses the Commission on Accreditation for Health Informatics and Information Management Education (CAHIIM) to provide premier program evaluation for health informatics education. CAHIIM accreditation demonstrates that academic standards are fulfilled to produce graduates who fulfill industry requirements. The accreditation of institutions by CAHIIM leads to high student confidence regarding educational quality and better prospects in the job market since employers tend to favor candidates from these accredited colleges Sapci and Sapci (2020a).

Students seeking CAHIIM-accredited master's degrees must complete their education through vital domains of health knowledge, social and behavioral sciences, human factors, leadership, and health information science. The thorough educational structure produces graduates who demonstrate competence in both technological aspects and interpersonal informatics settings (Mantas et al., 2010). By supporting the international recommendations set by IMIA, CAHIIM maintains a multidimensional educational approach by establishing educational results in clinical and managerial domains, along with technical domains.

Studying in any CAHIIM-approved program gives students entry to accreditation-based certifications, leading them to advanced careers and enhancing their professional standing. The seamless assessment of program validity is available straight from the CAHIIM site and through professional organizations, including AMIA and HIMSS.

Decoding Industry Certifications and Credentials

As a foundation, students can achieve with traditional degrees and increase their credibility through professional certifications that specialize in health informatics. The certification process proves competence in specific practice areas focused on the industry's professional standards.

The Registered Health Information Administrator (RHIA) represents among the most recognized qualifications in healthcare information administration. The RHIA credential comes from AHIMA and demands that graduates fulfill a bachelor's degree requirement from a CAHIIM-accredited program and pass the RHIA exam. RHIA professionals lead

EHR management and data governance activities and conduct compliance tasks (AMIA, 2008). As the second credential under AHIMA, the Registered Health Information Technician (RHIT) caters to associate degree holders who perform operational data work in healthcare facilities.

Professionals focusing on data reliability and regulatory standards should consider the Certified Health Data Analyst (CHDA) or the Certified in Healthcare Privacy and Security (CHPS) certifications. Healthcare roles in data breach response and big data implementation have become vital due to recent healthcare data security challenges (HIMSS, 2022).

HIMSS provides the Certified Professional in Healthcare Information and Management Systems (CPHIMS) and the lower-level Certified Associate in Healthcare Information and Management Systems (CAHIMS) for system-focused professionals. The certifications maintain international acceptance, and they address professionals who perform duties related to IT strategic planning, system implementation, and organizational leadership (Joe et al., 2011). Early-career professionals should begin with the less experienced-entry CAHIMS certification, while mid-level practitioners should focus on CPHIMS to build their expertise in health IT operations.

Physicians seeking clinical informatics certification should enroll at the American Board of Preventive Medicine because they officially recognize clinical informatics as a formal subspecialty. The certification requirement can be completed through an ACGME-accredited fellowship track or a work experience waiver system, as Hersh et al. (2022) described. Other professionals can earn the Advanced Health Informatics Certification (AHIC) from AMIA by holding a graduate degree and accumulating meaningful experience in informatics practice (Fridsma et al., 2016).

Your certification selection becomes easier when you know their requirements and purpose since this knowledge matches your expertise with future goals. Figure 3.1 offers a

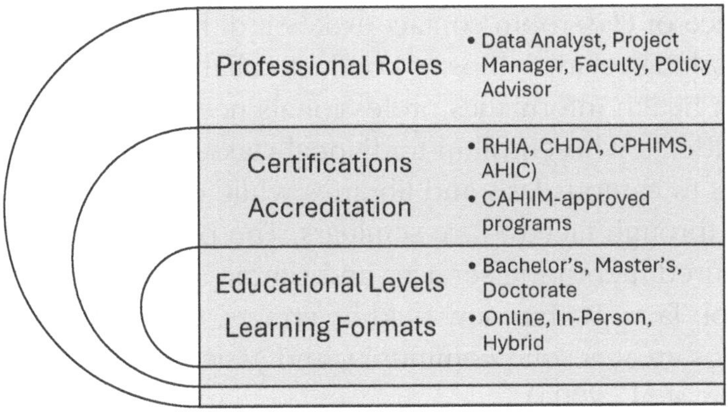

Figure 3.1 Educational and Credentialing Pathways in Health Informatics.

visual guide to educational and credentialing pathways, helping readers understand how formal education, accreditation, certification, and learning formats interconnect to support health informatics careers.

Online versus In-Person Learning: Flexibility Meets Structure

Your progress in a healthcare program depends heavily on whether it is taught online or in-person, together with hybrid learning options. Online programs' preference grows because they provide flexible education for working professionals who must manage several obligations with students from different countries. Learners can access asynchronous resources through these programs, which let them schedule their study time independently (Borycki et al., 2013).

The online learning format presents various obstacles to students. Virtual learning success requires students to demonstrate motivation, organizational skills, and technological expertise. The flexible learning mode works well, yet the absence of classroom contact makes it difficult to establish networking relationships or conduct collaborative work, which health informatics professionals need.

Students who enroll in traditional classes can have full access to campus labs and libraries while conducting group work through face-to-face seminars. The programs deliver structured mentoring services and simple access to internships and job fairs. Within new field beginners, the educational campus creates solid community and assistance networks (Green et al., 2004).

Programs with hybrid structures try to deliver features from traditional classroom learning alongside distance education benefits. The combination of virtual lectures with limited face-to-face meetings and in-person residency constitutes most of these programs. This program adapts to students who desire flexibility alongside occasional direct contact with others. Multiple CAHIIM-accredited universities have switched to hybrid education to address modern student diversity, according to Huang (2007).

Your choice of the correct format requires evaluating your learning methods, resource availability, and intended career path. Professional upskilling without disruption occurs best through online options, whereas traditional format education structures best support learners who want comprehensive, immersive learning.

Which Path Is Right for You?

Your optimum educational direction results from analyzing your life situation, professional goals, and personal conditions. The beginning of your career will benefit from earning a bachelor's degree in health informatics. The introductory healthcare data management or IT support positions become accessible through this educational pathway.

Those with healthcare or IT work experience or an existing degree may benefit from master's level training to enhance their career. The field welcomes master's degree holders for position opportunities in project management and clinical systems design, together with data analytic roles. People can become eligible to earn professional certifications, which include RHIA, CHDA, or CPHIMS, through these programs.

Doctoral degree programs provide the best option for people interested in shaping healthcare through research, executive leadership, or developing healthcare policies. PhD graduates commonly establish their careers as faculty teachers, research principal investigators, and senior informatics professionals. The future direction of the discipline is formed by these expertise and innovative approaches (Borycki et al., 2013).

The decision depends on your reflection about your learning style, professional planning, and how the choice aligns with your career trajectory. I need to determine whether I want flexibility or need structure in my career. My interests lie in analyzing data, implementing systems, and developing policies for production. What basic qualifications are required to obtain my professional objectives?

Summary and Reflection

The educational routes to study health informatics represent the same diversity in the field. Health Informatics programs from bachelor to master and doctoral levels provide separate advantages that match professional goals at various career points. The leading indicator for excellent educational quality is understanding the importance of receiving CAHIIM accreditation. Multiple industry-based qualifications, including RHIA, CHDA, CPHIMS, and AHIC, bolster your professional reputation and career growth potential.

Your study choice between online and campus learning matters less than your ability to attain goals both personally and professionally. Your decision to invest in appropriate healthcare data education creates career benefits and opportunities to advance critical patient care approaches and public health advancement. Our upcoming chapter discusses how the acquired education serves as a basis to obtain entry-level position opportunities where you can implement what you learned.

Chapter 4

Entry-Level Roles in Health Informatics

After pursuing an education in Healthcare Informatics, it is the right time to get insight into career opportunities and beginner roles for kickstarting the professional journey. As you walk through this chapter, you will discover a whole new world of possibilities for beginners, such as data analytics, management, abstraction, etc. As you spend time as a beginner, you will learn to grow and innovate to explore more opportunities. Here are the details of the chapter.

The Entry-Level Roles of Health Informatics Provide Opportunities for Beginners

The transition into health informatics comes with excitement and overwhelming challenges. Combining healthcare services with data management and technological capabilities presents a special field opportunity for professionals. The content about entry-level health informatics roles enables you to establish your course after joining the workforce directly from

DOI: 10.4324/9781003689843-4

Figure 4.1 Entry-Level Career Pathways in Health Informatics.

school or changing professions or as an international professional moving to the United States (Clarke et al., 2016; Haghi et al., 2017; Patel, 2019). This section offers entry-stage job descriptions for health informatics positions by explaining their functions while detailing necessary qualifications and projected job market directions. Figure 4.1 provides a career pathway roadmap for entry-level health informatics professionals. It visually demonstrates how foundational education leads to specific job roles, certifications, and career advancement.

Understanding Entry-Level Health Informatics Roles

New healthcare informaticians create their digital health career foundation through entry-level positions (Hersh, 2021; Luo et al., 2016). EHR management and data analysis work alongside clinical documentation integrity to make up fundamental health informatics operations. Health informatics organizations deploy consistent fundamental roles among their workforce, but they clarify different job posts throughout various institutions.

As a Health Informatics Analyst, you must obtain health data through standardized practices for subsequent evaluation and interpretation, supporting medical and administrative functions (Kaplan, 2020; Mackert et al., 2016; Shickel et al., 2017). These healthcare professionals use EHR systems while needing expertise in data visualization techniques and SQL database querying skills. Many analysts transition into their current positions through clinical and non-technical backgrounds by completing short-term certifications along with intensive boot camp programs, as reported by Lee et al. (2024). Their professional duties include the preparation of dashboards, data quality reporting, and supporting research activities requiring patient data summary tasks.

The Health Information Management (HIM) technician maintains patient records through the essential duties of accuracy alongside confidentiality and record integrity protection. The practitioner must apply ICD-10 and CPT codes to diagnose and provide procedural information. Medical records custodianship is a core responsibility of HIM technicians who maintain data compliance through policy enforcement. According to Gibson et al. (2015), the HIM technical role goes beyond standard documentation to perform digital content management with data quality auditing tasks.

Research environments at academic medical centers and clinical trial facilities heavily depend on clinical data coordinators for operational success. This professional group's role entails data input, management, and source data collection. The role demands precision and quickness from clinical data coordinators because the position links research teams to electronic data capture systems, according to Fang et al. (2016). Research coordinators must have comprehensive knowledge of regulations, including Good Clinical Practice (GCP) and the Health Insurance Portability and Accountability Act (HIPAA).

The responsibilities of data abstractors include extracting pertinent clinical information from patient charts and records, which serve quality reporting needs, audit functions, and research requirements. Many healthcare organizations activate abstractors for population health projects because these professionals collect aggregated information spanning multiple patient treatment periods, according to McLane et al. (2021). Both detail-oriented skills and mastery of data interpretation apply to abstractors who work with structured and unstructured EHR system data. Table 4.1 presents a comparison of common entry-level roles in Health Informatics. It

Table 4.1 Entry-Level Health Informatics Roles

Role Title	*Primary Responsibilities*	*Required Skills/ Qualifications*	*Average Starting Salary*
Health Informatics Analyst	Data analysis, dashboard creation, trend reporting, EHR querying	Bachelor's or grad certificate, SQL, Tableau, communication	$60,000–$75,000
HIM Technician	Medical coding, documentation accuracy, record integrity, compliance	Associate or Bachelor's, ICD-10/CPT coding, RHIT	$45,000–$60,000
Clinical Data Coordinator	Clinical trial data entry, source documentation, regulatory compliance	Bachelor's, REDCap/ Medidata, GCP, HIPAA	$50,000–$65,000
Data Abstractor	Extract clinical data, support audits and QI projects	Bachelor's, abstraction tools, HEDIS/CORE knowledge	$50,000–$65,000

outlines responsibilities, required skills, and average salary ranges, helping readers understand the distinctions and expectations of each position.

Typical Responsibilities and Required Skillsets

Newcomer positions in healthcare require employees to combine specific technical capabilities with professional expertise and strong relational abilities. The job involves Health Informatics Analysts with analytical thinking capabilities and comfort using Excel, SQL, and Tableau data tools. Nurses specializing in data analysis must fully comprehend clinical workflows and patient-specific medical terminology since these elements strongly shape data collection interpretation and utilization (Lee et al., 2024). Organizations currently focus on hiring candidates who transform data insights into supporting both clinical and administrative decisions.

Workers in this job need distinct abilities from those required in other healthcare information positions. Medical coders must demonstrate competency, while IT professionals need skills handling health information systems and expertise in privacy standards. The training of technicians has expanded to include modern digital workflow skills for document scanning and hybrid record management with metadata tagging processes, according to Gibson et al. (2015). His technicians must demonstrate expertise in collaborating with nurses, physicians, and IT personnel through interdisciplinary teams.

The main requirement for clinical data coordinators is to pay close attention to every detail of their work. Clinical data coordinators manage extensive sensitive information within REDCap and Medidata Rave databases through precise and efficient operations, according to Fang et al. (2016). The success of these professionals demands strict adherence to protocols while they also need complete mastery of clinical trial design aspects.

The role of data abstractors requires great clinical expertise and expertise in multiple documentation platforms. The role of data abstraction necessitates healthcare providers to analyze physician documentation to obtain crucial information for quality reports. According to Fitzmaurice et al. (2002), abstractors are essential contributors to performance measurement and quality improvement programs. Knowledge regarding abstraction software and HEDIS or CORE standards is advantageous for work success.

Salary Expectations and Job Outlook

According to information from the U.S. Bureau of Labor Statistics and HIMSS job vacancies, first-year health informatics positions reflect a favorable compensation range and job potential. The annual earnings for Health Informatics Analysts fall between $60,000 and $75,000, though geographic location and specific institutions influence this range. Academic medical centers and large health systems offer better initial compensation because of their complicated data and reporting structures (Ma, 2020).

HIM technicians receive starting salaries between $45,000 and $60,000 annually in their initial positions. Certification in coding or privacy creates specialized opportunities that allow healthcare information technicians grow their salaries and establish themselves as leaders (Gibson et al., 2015).

Clinical data coordinators earn salaries comparable to HIM technicians, yet they might receive elevated pay when working in research-driven pharmaceutical or healthcare organizations. Working on federally funded research projects grants employees both stipends and bonuses through grant cycles and regulatory milestone achievements, according to McLane et al. (2021).

Employees who work as data abstractors generally receive salaries from $50,000 to $65,000 annually. Data abstractors receive salary variations that depend upon their employment status, whether full-time, part-time, or based on contract agreements. The demand for abstractors has increased because CMS and other regulatory agencies enforce value-based care reporting mandates (Hoyt et al., 2007).

These career roles expect a favorable job market prospect in the future. Healthcare data informatics will experience an anticipated growth of 16% from 2022 to 2032 because healthcare organizations need expanded data resources, new healthcare standards, and the adoption of digital healthcare technology in care service delivery (McLane et al., 2021). Hiring organizations today seek employees with technological proficiency and precise knowledge of healthcare delivery systems.

A Day in the Life: Health Informatics Analyst

Amira's career starts today as she enters her first day working as a Health Informatics Analyst at a big community hospital. She begins her day by meeting with colleagues to review work-related issues assigned by the Quality Improvement team. Each month, the QI team requires readmission rate assessments separated by diagnosis-related groups in a monthly format. Before visualizing hospital trends during the past six months, Amira retrieves EHR information through SQL and uses Tableau software for visualization.

She teams up with clinical staff members to develop precise data definitions about a new performance metric focused on sepsis care. She uses her clinical experience to grasp data documentation factors determining data reliability. She devotes her afternoon to a virtual interoperability session organized by the state health information exchange system. She dedicates the last part of her day to modifying a department-wide dashboard that monitors medication reconciliation compliance.

The postgraduate certificate in health informatics allowed Amira to execute communication skill sets, analysis techniques, and documentation strategies, which she uses throughout her daily responsibilities. Through her work, she experiences fulfillment because her contributions directly influence patient care and organizational decision processes (Lee et al., 2024).

Education and Certification Pathways

The minimum entry-level positions in healthcare have different educational benchmarks. Individuals should possess a bachelor's degree in Health Information Management, Health Informatics, or a related discipline to qualify for HIM technicians and data abstractors positions. Analysts and clinical data coordinators obtain better career outcomes by obtaining graduate certifications in data analytics or public health (Ma, 2020; Fitzmaurice et al., 2002).

The Registered Health Information Technician (RHIT), Certified Health Data Analyst (CHDA), and Certified Associate in Healthcare Information and Management Systems (CAHIMS) certifications represent highly beneficial qualifications for this field. Research from Hoyt et al. (2007) shows that contemporary business organizations seek job applicants who actively pursue education and professional development.

Health information system professionals seeking career transition through medical informatics can benefit from the intensive AMIA 10x10 short-term training program. Such programs supply students with the essential knowledge base and hands-on abilities, thus streamlining their professional transition process (Lee et al., 2024).

Summary and Reflection

Health informatics continues to expand, which creates new career possibilities for people starting their careers. All three domains of data analysis, information governance, and clinical documentation have roles available in the field that you can pursue. Before obtaining certifications and the required educational qualifications, you should learn the expectations and skill sets.

Every beginner should dedicate time for introspection to determine the entry-level position that suits their abilities and passions. Is coding and classification system design something that brings you joy? Workers with an interest in medical documentation should consider HIM technician duties. Data analysis alongside visualization appeals to you more than other areas of work. A position as an informatics analyst should be your choice for career entry. Knowing your preferences allows you to match them with healthcare industry needs, thus creating a straightforward path to career success.

Chapter 5

Advanced Career Opportunities

Welcome to the exciting prospects of mid- to senior-level job roles in health informatics, which would be your dream career. These leadership positions and roles allow you to innovate, apply change management, and drive the path toward excellence and quality in healthcare. Whether you aspire to become a clinical informatics specialist, CMIO, CIO, or product manager, this chapter will provide the requisite knowledge and information to apply in the respective field. Your journey as a healthcare informatics leader and manager starts here with sufficient details to leap.

Embracing Leadership in Health Informatics

Modern health informatics expanded its origins in medical technology applications into becoming essential healthcare personnel (Fridsma, 2019; Ognjanović et al., 2024; Rajamani et al., 2024). Health informatics professionals at mid- to senior-levels

 DOI: 10.4324/9781003689843-5

now have chances to enhance their career development while directly influencing healthcare delivery efficiency and patient outcomes as the healthcare sector continues its innovative progress. The following section explores advanced healthcare career options such as clinical informatics specialist, consultant, chief medical information officer (CMIO), chief information officer (CIO), and product manager. Combining leadership with expertise and innovative qualities drives these professional roles toward future healthcare development.

These roles offer insight into high-level health informatics success criteria and position you effectively within this fast-growing industry. Figure 5.1 illustrates the professional development trajectory for advanced health informatics careers, highlighting the pathway from mid-level expertise through strategic specialization to executive leadership.

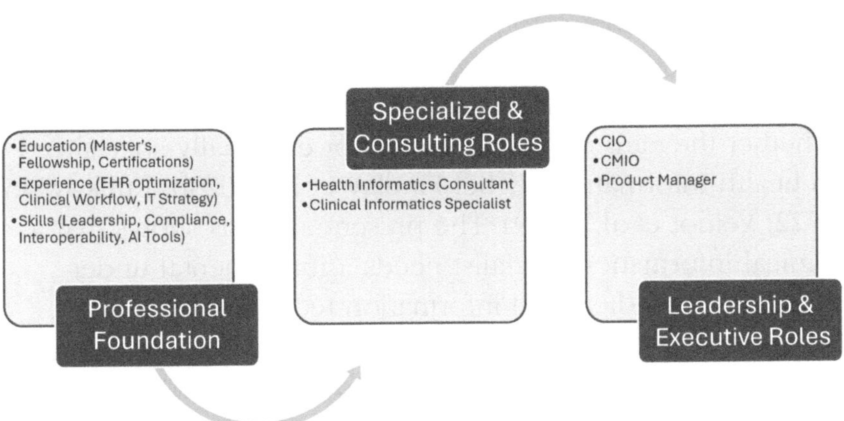

Figure 5.1 Health Informatics Leadership and Career Progression Pathway.

Clinical Informatics Specialist: Transforming Patient Care through Technology

A clinical informatics specialist maintains the vital function of bringing information technology smoothly into clinical healthcare operations. Healthcare organizations actively search for this role because they depend on electronic health record (EHR) systems and other health technologies to achieve better clinical results. Health information systems gain their full potential from clinical informatics specialists who create them and make them functional for clinical staff usage daily (Cummins et al., 2016; Kim, 2017; Rudolf et al., 2018). The specialists collaborate extensively with medical staff, nursing personnel, and other healthcare providers to confirm the technology appropriately supports clinical work procedures, leading to optimal patient care.

Required Experience and Responsibilities

Effective performance as a clinical informatics specialist requires practitioners to possess a thorough knowledge of clinical operations and a strong command of IT systems. Most CIS professionals come from healthcare backgrounds, whether they are nurses or doctors or eventually specialized in health informatics (Bichel-Findlay et al., 2023b; Kulikowski, 2022; Veinot et al., 2019). The present analysis shows that a clinical informatics specialist needs a fundamental understanding of medical and information technology elements since health information exchange software and clinical decision support systems form the foundation for successful performance (Hoyt et al., 2020). The professional duties of CIS professionals extend to optimizing EHR system usage while enhancing system usability, delivering training sessions for clinicians, and addressing technical problems that emerge in clinical settings.

The healthcare professional must demonstrate mastery of HIPAA and meaningful use criteria alongside regulatory requirements since these standards help medical organizations meet data privacy legislation and improve care (McLane et al., 2021). Clinical decision support systems require clinical informatics specialists to develop them to make evidence-based clinical choices directly available to care providers (Masuda, 2008).

Career Outlook

Healthcare organizations will experience substantial growth in their need for clinical informatics specialists because they continue integrating new technological solutions. Health informatics roles will substantially expand by more than 15% during the next decade, according to the projections by the U.S. Bureau of Labor Statistics (BLS) (2021). Healthcare is undergoing digitalization alongside a rising need for data-based clinical decision-making, which is driving this growth (Masuda, 2008; Middleton et al., 2014). The growing need for healthcare professionals who can mediate between providers and healthcare technology becomes essential because the aging population and the ever-increasing telemedicine and mobile solutions of the healthcare industry demand it.

Health Informatics Consultant: Guiding Healthcare Organizations through Technological Change

Specialists known as health informatics consultants show healthcare organizations the path to achieve maximum efficiency from their health IT systems. Health informatics consultants assist hospitals in selecting appropriate EHR systems while developing digital health strategies for healthcare providers through diverse tasks and challenges. The health informatics consultant's role suits individuals who appreciate diverse work experiences because they support different clients operating within various organizational settings.

Required Experience and Responsibilities

Experienced consultants in health informatics must demonstrate mastery of healthcare and IT disciplines. The experts have completed their studies in health informatics degrees along with similar fields and demonstrate extensive experience dealing with health IT system implementations, workflow improvements, and data studies (Slight & Moore, 2021). As part of their duties, consultants must determine which system technologies suit a healthcare organization's needs through system evaluations to help choose and deploy suitable health IT solutions.

Consultants take charge of training and change management activities as they work to help organizations adjust properly to their new systems. Due to their role, consultants need exceptional analytical and problem-solving abilities to evaluate health organizations separately before developing customized improvements for clinical and operational results (McLane et al., 2021).

Career Outlook

Health informatics consulting allows professionals to create work schedules and immense professional income possibilities. The job market seeks health informatics consultants with expertise in system integration, data management, and process optimization functions. The consultant profession will expand exceptionally because organizations need external experts to handle digital transformation complexities. General IT consultancy employment, including healthcare specialties, will grow at a 10% rate throughout the upcoming ten years, as predicted by BLS (2021). This career exists because of its diverse technical tasks, attracting people who like to solve problems daily.

Chief Medical Information Officer (CMIO): Leading the Integration of Technology and Healthcare

Clinical expertise and informatics expertise define the executive management requirements of a chief medical information officer position. CMIOs lead the process of integrating health information technology into clinical practice, which results in IT systems that deliver both patient care and healthcare delivery capabilities. As healthcare professionals, they oversee the strategy to implement and maximize the potential of clinical information systems throughout operational healthcare institutions.

Required Experience and Responsibilities

The team leader possessing the CMIO title represents medical professionals who gained expertise through medical practice and obtained qualifications in health informatics or healthcare information technology. CMIOs require clinical experience with leadership capabilities to run cross-functional teams, create strategic choices, and deliver effective messages to executive leaders, according to Hoyt et al. (2020). EHR system implementation falls within their scope of work alongside workflow optimization, regulatory compliance, and the task of leading health organizations in implementing artificial intelligence and telemedicine solutions.

Executive team members, including the CMIO and CIO, collaborate to ensure that clinical technology supports organizational goals. Healthcare professionals rely on CMIOs to represent their needs before organizations and to instruct them regarding efficient digital health system usage. The primary duty of CMIOs includes maintaining cyber safety abilities while verifying that EHR systems fulfill clinical requirements, optimizing workflows, and generating positive patient outcomes (Slight & Moore, 2021).

Career Outlook

Healthcare organizations maintain digital health as their primary focus, which makes CMIO positions more vital than ever. CMIO positions will experience growing demand because of the general advancement in health IT activities, which include decision-making systems that use advanced technologies and data analytics. According to the BLS research, CMIO positions will become one of the most needed leadership roles in health IT over the next ten years (BLS, 2021). This job compiles incredible power to shape healthcare policy while unifying new technological implementations and advancing patient care delivery, which positions it as having the most effective role in health informatics.

Chief Information Officer (CIO): Overseeing Health IT Strategy at the Executive Level

Healthcare organizations depend on chief information officers (CIOs) to direct their complete IT operational strategies from an executive position. As a CIO, the responsibility extends beyond clinical technology to complete management control of administrative systems, cybersecurity, and other organizational IT infrastructure. CIOs maintain a crucial role during technology strategy development since they help execute strategies according to organizational objectives.

Required Experience and Responsibilities

Most chief information officers have IT or business administrative experience as their background. Working professionals in IT management possess business and advanced IT education while demonstrating extensive experience managing big IT operations. McLane et al. (2021) explain that CIOs need experience with healthcare operational understanding since their purpose involves connecting technology systems to clinical and business needs. As part of their responsibilities, the CIO team guarantees IT systems' protection and expandability, including patient portals alongside enterprise resource planning (ERP) systems.

The CIO collaborates with the CMIO to ensure that health IT systems fulfill their clinical requirements. The CIO directs budget management while leading teams through staff administration and guides their organization through technology implementation such as big data analytics, cloud computing, and AI tools. Modern CEOs require leadership abilities and project management expertise to thrive in the profession, as Masuda (2008) has noted.

Career Outlook

Healthcare institutions need CIO leadership for their digital transformation success to succeed. Healthcare institutions will intensify their search for highly experienced IT executives because of the growing technology dependency in healthcare, thus ensuring demand growth for CIO positions. The BLS reports that IT executives face high demand, and healthcare organizations especially seek CIOs capable of managing extensive digital transformations (BLS, 2021).

Product Manager in Health Informatics: Developing Digital Health Solutions

Health informatics product managers direct all stages of development by releasing digital health products such as EHR systems, mobile health applications, and telemedicine platforms. By merging their business understanding with technical knowledge, they guarantee that products provide the needed user experience and fulfill regulatory demands while enhancing healthcare service delivery.

Required Experience and Responsibilities

Healthcare expertise alongside business or technological background defines the background of product managers. A product manager executes three primary functions, which include developing product vision statements and handling project development phases to maintain market-compatible product features. Health informatics product managers require excellent leadership and communication abilities, according to McLane et al. (2021), because they work directly with such teams as development and, marketing and clinical personnel. A product manager must understand the healthcare market regulatory requirements and have knowledge and experience in user-centered design principles.

Product managers have essential duties: directing product growth through development stages up to market release, collecting end-user input for analysis, and dealing with compliance with healthcare rules. The collaboration between product managers, clinical staff, IT professionals, and business leaders serves to develop functional products that meet organizational targets (Hoyt et al., 2020).

Career Outlook

Health informatics organizations expand their recruitment of product managers because they need digital solutions to improve patient healthcare quality. The BLS anticipates quick growth in product management positions across technology and healthcare sectors, while specialists focusing on health informatics will find great success. This role combines technical skills with managerial expertise and strategic development abilities to allow professionals who want to influence digital health transformation.

Summary and Reflection

Health informatics professionals have multiple exciting career opportunities, ranging from clinical informatics specialists to product managers, enabling them to drive meaningful healthcare advancements. Table 5.1 compares advanced health informatics roles across key responsibilities, required qualifications, and career outlook. It provides a strategic overview for professionals considering leadership and specialized roles. High-level health informatics positions demand professionals with expertise in technology leadership abilities and strategic planning knowledge. Organizations will continue adopting digital transformation in healthcare, expanding opportunities for skilled professionals in these roles. Healthcare professionals with appropriate qualifications, experience, and the necessary mindset can acquire leadership roles to build healthcare delivery's future.

Table 5.1 Comparison of Advanced Health Informatics Roles

Role Title	*Key Responsibilities*	*Required Experience/ Skills*	*Career Outlook*
Clinical Informatics Specialist	Integrate EHR systems, optimize workflows, support clinical staff	Clinical background, health IT skills, HIPAA, CDS systems	High demand: +15% growth expected due to EHR expansion
Health Informatics Consultant	Advise on HIT implementation, system selection, change management	Health IT experience, problem-solving, training delivery, analytics	Growing demand for external transformation experts (+10% projected)
Chief Medical Information Officer (CMIO)	Lead clinical IT strategy, optimize digital care delivery	Physician background, leadership, health IT, AI, compliance	High-value leadership role with long-term growth potential
Chief Information Officer (CIO)	Oversee entire health IT infrastructure, manage IT strategy and budgets	IT/business leadership, healthcare knowledge, cybersecurity	High demand due to digital transformation in healthcare
Product Manager (Health IT)	Lead development of EHRs, apps, and digital tools from concept to market	Healthcare, IT/ business experience, UX, regulatory knowledge	Rapidly growing with strong career advancement potential

Chapter 6

Emerging Trends and Future Directions

The future of health informatics is bright and moving toward innovative directions that seek your attention and exploration to pursue your career in it. Due to the rise in AI and ML in different sectors and industries, healthcare intervention methods are also advancing to minimize human interventions and approach innovative methods to optimize the quality of care.

Introduction: The Future Is Now

Healthcare stands at the beginning of a transformative era, which is what emerging technologies bring to care delivery systems while also getting better patient results. Health informatics is moving forward with revolutionary changes because of combined efforts between artificial intelligence (AI), machine learning (ML), telehealth, big data, blockchain, and natural language processing (NLP) (Gu et al., 2019; Monkman et al., 2023). Emerging technologies transform existing roles and generate fresh career paths that bring

DOI: 10.4324/9781003689843-6

Table 6.1 Emerging Technologies in Health Informatics

Technology	*Primary Function*	*Impact on Healthcare*	*Emerging Careers*
Artificial Intelligence (AI) and Machine Learning (ML)	Predictive analytics, diagnostic support, personalized medicine	Improved diagnostics, real-time decisions, enhanced treatment accuracy	AI Specialist, Clinical Decision Support Developer
Telehealth and Remote Monitoring	Virtual consultations, chronic disease monitoring	Expanded access, reduced hospital visits, patient engagement	Telehealth Coordinator, Virtual Care Manager
Big Data	Large-scale data analysis and forecasting	Resource optimization, population health insights, cost savings	Healthcare Data Scientist, Predictive Modeler
Blockchain	Secure data exchange and immutable recordkeeping	Enhanced data privacy, interoperability, fraud prevention	Blockchain Architect, Health Data Security Engineer
Natural Language Processing (NLP)	Interpretation of unstructured clinical text and voice data	Automated documentation, clinical insights, efficiency gains	NLP Developer, Clinical Documentation Analyst

attractive professional opportunities to health informatics specialists. The healthcare field shows great promise through future growth because individuals who maintain innovative leadership positions with newly adapted tools and continuous learning will be essential to this evolution. The following section analyzes current health informatics trends and future development possibilities, examines operational technologies, and demonstrates upcoming career directions in this changing industry domain. Table 6.1 highlights key emerging technologies in health informatics, their primary functions, and their impact on healthcare delivery and professional opportunities. It provides a snapshot of innovations shaping the future.

The Role of AI and ML in Health Informatics

The fundamental components of contemporary health informatics consist of artificial intelligence and machine learning because these fields enable the transformation of diagnostic algorithms, treatment protocol design, and patient therapeutic services (Demiris, 2016; Gülkesen & Haux, 2019; Orji & Moffatt, 2018). Through AI algorithms, a massive amount of healthcare data can be processed to reveal new patterns and predictions that were impossible to achieve. Deep learning models show exceptional accuracy during abnormality detection in radiology images because they surpass human radiologists (Jiang et al., 2017). Machine learning boosts clinical decision support systems through patient-specific recommendations during real-time treatments, which leads to better treatment decisions and healthcare results.

The inclusion of AI and ML into clinical practice faces challenges despite recently achieved innovations. Integrating AI into clinical practice faces substantial challenges because healthcare organizations need to solve problems related to data privacy, algorithm bias, and requirements for transparent AI decisions (Murthy, 2022; Tortorella et al., 2020). Healthcare professional trust decreases when "black-box" models hide their decision-making processes from view because it interferes with their adoption of these systems (Kohane, 2019). Adopting ethical, transparent, and equitable AI healthcare systems will require technologists to work with clinicians and policy-makers permanently.

Telehealth and Remote Patient Monitoring: A New Era of Care

Telehealth combined with remote patient monitoring systems became a major healthcare element after the onset of the COVID-19 pandemic. The technology enables healthcare providers to treat patients without access to standard face-to-face visits because of geographic or physical limitations. Through video consultations, patients can obtain professional medical guidance from their homes. Besides telehealth, remote patient monitoring exists, which adopts devices to measure vital signs and chronic conditions to provide ongoing healthcare data to providers, ensuring improved patient health management (Dorsey et al., 2016).

Telehealth expansion has substantially broadened medical service provision while filling gaps in rural parts of the country alongside underserved patient populations. The healthcare system operates more efficiently because telehealth has decreased the demands of hospital emergency departments and clinic outpatients. The continuous increase of telehealth service requirements generates parallel growing requirements for professional personnel who oversee telehealth frameworks and maintain security protocols while integrating these systems into healthcare systems.

Big Data and Blockchain: Transforming Health Information Management

Health information management can find transformative potential through big data and blockchain. Healthcare delivery benefits from big data analytics because the system collects substantial healthcare data from multiple sources, which allows users to reveal patterns and trends that enhance healthcare service quality. Big data delivers essential insights that help healthcare institutions make evidence-based decisions through its ability to forecast disease spreads and optimize resource management (Tuckson et al., 2017).

Many health data management challenges will find solutions through blockchain technology because it delivers protected and transparent yet indestructible healthcare records. Through blockchain-enabled secure patient information distribution between medical providers, the system improves cross-disciplinary data exchange while always guaranteeing access to precise, up-to-date medical records (Salem, 2022). The blockchain network acts as an enhancement for healthcare data privacy through secure and immutable recordkeeping, which resolves issues related to healthcare data breaches and unauthorized access to sensitive patient information.

Natural Language Processing: Unlocking the Power of Clinical Data

Health informatics benefits strongly from transformative natural language processing (NLP) technology. Healthy data interpretation becomes possible through Natural Language Processing because this technology enables computers to understand spoken language. This makes clinical research accessible through unorganized healthcare documents, including physician notes, patient files, and research publications. Implementing NLP-powered systems enables analysis of these documents toward discovering important data and automated administration functionalities and clinical decision support.

NLP systems have already normalized the automatic extraction process for essential data points from electronic health records (EHRs), and this frees clinicians time to deliver better patient care (Jiang et al., 2017). The application of NLP enables the identification of repetitive patterns in clinical documentation that may indicate future disease risks or potential complications. NLP technology development will power up the efficiency and accuracy of healthcare delivery practices at an accelerated pace.

The Watchlist: Careers of the Future in Health Informatics

Several new work possibilities are developing within health informatics thanks to advancements in the healthcare field. The future of healthcare needs qualified individuals to work with AI, ML, telehealth, big data, blockchain, and NLP because these technologies advance into medical systems. Health informatics professionals will pursue promising careers, which include:

- Medical professionals specializing in AI algorithms will develop programs that produce clinical decision-making solutions and diagnostic instrumentation, among other health applications.
- Managers and coordinators of telehealth services must rise to meet emerging demands since healthcare institutions require experts to control their platforms while maintaining regulatory standards and improving patient experience.
- Healthcare data analysis by data scientists and analysts enables them to discover improvements in patient care, operation optimization, and cost reduction.

- Blockchain developers' goal will be to design and implement blockchain solutions to enable healthcare organizations to secure their data management while streamlining operations.
- Clinical data extraction and decision-enhancing functions become achievable through NLP experts who streamline administrative operations.

Figure 6.1 provides a visual map of emerging health informatics trends and their corresponding career pathways. It demonstrates how modern technologies give rise to new roles while shaping strategic future directions.

Potential Disruptions and How to Stay Ahead of the Curve

Health informatics continues to undergo quick technological transformations that generate spontaneous industry changes.

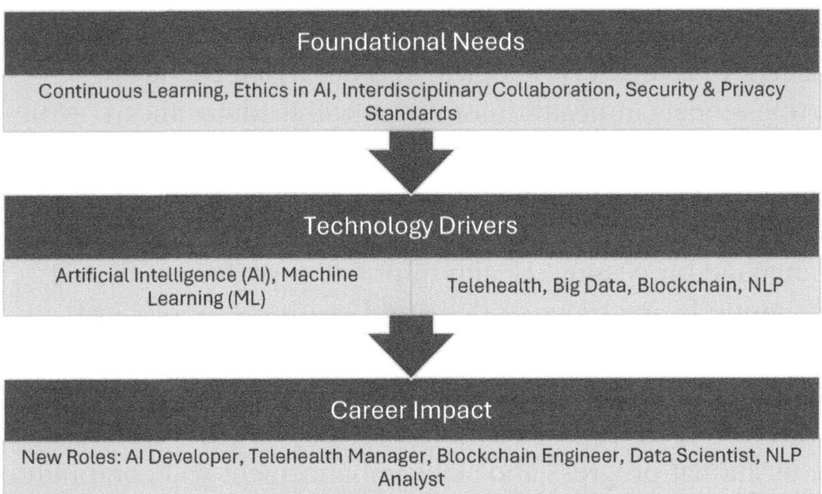

Figure 6.1 Future-Focused Trends and Career Pathways in Health Informatics.

Healthcare technologies deliver abundant opportunities yet present several problems, including robotic workplace substitution while maintaining employee roles, protecting personal information, and addressing the moral aspects of machine learning system decisions. Professionals must practice ongoing learning to become leaders by staying updated with modern trends and mastering the foundational expertise of developing healthcare technologies.

Healthcare professionals must acquire excellent collaboration abilities because combining these technologies demands cooperation between providers, technologists, data scientists, and policy-makers to achieve integration. Through their work toward developing an innovative team mindset, they ensure that these technologies serve their intended purpose: improving patient health outcomes and care quality.

Summary and Reflection

The future of health informatics appears promising because dedicated professionals can prosper through their ability to accept evolving technological and approach changes. Professionals in health informatics will lead healthcare evolution and improve patient success rates by accepting emerging technologies, including artificial intelligence, machine learning and telehealth, data science, blockchain systems, and natural language processing. Health informatics professionals will continue facing growing demand because technological evolution predicts an increased need for experts who can master advanced healthcare solutions and tackle obstacles to advance innovation. Health informatics experts who maintain educational progress and skills enhancement will contribute to the medical industry's evolution throughout the upcoming years.

Chapter 7

Navigating the Job Market

Your success in health informatics employment requires specific plans to differentiate your candidacy from qualified competitors. The chapter instructs readers about fundamental job search steps, including resume development with cover letters, interview preparation, and networking connections. The fast-growing nature of health informatics enables individuals to build successful careers through proper approaches. A successful health informatics career can be achieved by matching your application materials to industry requirements while improving your networking methods.

Resume and Cover Letter Strategies with Keyword Optimization

To succeed in health informatics, you must develop documents showcasing your special expertise and professional characteristics. Job candidates in health informatics must utilize ATS systems for screening, so their resumes need to

DOI: 10.4324/9781003689843-7

contain job description-compatible keywords to pass filtrations successfully. Research shows that the main health informatics terms to incorporate on your resume are "electronic health records (EHR)," "clinical data management," "health IT systems," "HIPAA compliance," and "data governance" (Jiang et al., 2017; Bossen et al., 2019). The technology-related vocabulary in your resume enables employer match-ups and permits ATS system assessment of your document.

The cover letter demonstrates your knowledge of employer needs by displaying applicable qualifications and the candidate's passion for the position. Each cover letter should directly reference a company's objectives and display your qualifications for helping the organization reach its goals. Your technical expertise in analysis or electronic health record systems needs a clear demonstration of their operational benefits for patient services alongside operational efficiency (Sharp et al., 2020).

Health informatics professionals demand practical experience working with particular software applications and technical tools to successfully obtain their roles (Sharp et al., 2020). Your job market value will improve through demonstrating technical skills with Tableau, SQL, Cerner, and Epic software (Madlock-Brown et al., 2021).

Common Interview Questions for Health Informatics Roles

Health informatics interviews consist of technical questions and behavioral questions. Your careful preparation of answers for these interview questions will produce the confidence you need to do well. Some common interview questions include the following.

Please Describe Your Experience of using Analytics to Find Solutions for Healthcare Issues

The patient admission patterns project at my previous position required my leadership while using SQL and Tableau platforms. Our team discovered delayed processes in the emergency department, so we transformed patient admission protocols to shorten emergency room waiting periods by 20%.

Please Explain Your Data Security Methods for Health Informatics Systems

Handling sensitive patient information has become my top priority because I strictly follow HIPAA guidelines. In my previous workplace, I implemented data encryption strategies for data storage plus transmission, which secured full adherence to state and federal regulatory rules.

Describe How You Handled a Health IT Solution Implementation with Personnel from Different Functional Departments

My team implemented the new EHR system by working with IT specialists, clinicians, and administrators. Establishing open communication links and stakeholder training enabled us to shift to the new system effortlessly, thus enhancing workflow efficiency for clinical work.

Technical ability and interpersonal skills must be demonstrated in your responses because these questions evaluate whether you can make technology accessible to healthcare staff (Masuda, 2008; Sharp et al., 2020).

Job Boards: HIMSS JobMine, AHIMA, LinkedIn, HealthITJobs.com

Job seekers must use specialized health informatics professional job boards as they represent crucial resources for their job search (Alherz et al., 2025; Lee et al., 2024). Job platforms present filtering systems that enable users to find suitable opportunities by matching their experience with geographical areas and work role choices. Key job boards include:

- HIMSS JobMine is a prime platform for health IT job posts, providing professionals across health informatics, EHR implementation, and data analysis access to thousands of job listings. The health informatics field depends on HIMSS to locate skilled candidates, according to Bossen et al. (2019).
- AHIMA Career Center presents health information management professionals with a comprehensive job-search platform targeting healthcare positions in information management, clinical informatics, and data analytics. AHIMA provides job-specific resources and professional development tools that help develop your skills, leading to career success in the healthcare sector (Madlock-Brown et al., 2021).
- Business professionals should utilize LinkedIn because it allows them to capture essential networking and career opportunities. Through LinkedIn, many businesses display available job positions for candidates, while job seekers can establish direct connections with executives who perform hiring roles and leaders from their target industries. When optimized LinkedIn profiles function as digital resumes, they display your skills, accomplishments, and professional networking connections (Masuda, 2008).
- The dedicated health IT job board at HealthITJobs.com serves directly as an excellent platform for professionals

who specialize in health informatics. The site delivers contemporary job listings that help job seekers identify positions in health data management IT systems and telemedicine fields.

The job boards serve as essential resources for candidates who want to reach employers who base their hiring criteria on health informatics specialization (Jiang et al., 2017). Table 7.1 summarizes strategic components of the job search

Table 7.1 Job Search Strategies for Health Informatics Professionals

Category	*Key Strategies*	*Tools/ Platforms*	*Professional Tips*
Resume & Cover Letter	Keyword optimization, role-specific content, quantifiable outcomes	ATS, Word, PDF Editors	Include terms like EHR, HIPAA, SQL, and Tableau
Interview Preparation	Prepare for technical + behavioral questions, highlight impact	STAR Method, Mock Interviews	Use examples that show collaboration, innovation, and measurable results
Job Boards	Targeted applications, filter by role/location/ keywords	HIMSS JobMine, AHIMA, LinkedIn, HealthITJobs.com	Set job alerts and apply to 5–10 positions weekly
Networking & Associations	Engage on LinkedIn, join professional associations, attend events	HIMSS, AMIA, AHIMA, Webinars, LinkedIn	Follow up after events; seek informational interviews

process in health informatics, including best practices for resumes, interviews, networking, and job board utilization to improve your career outcomes.

Networking Tips and Leveraging Professional Associations

Using your network effectively constitutes the strongest way to advance your health informatics career. The cooperativeness of the field requires strong professional relationships because they help you uncover job chances and understand industry developments (Alzghaibi, 2023; Elnoshokaty et al., 2023). Health informatics professionals gain access to networking opportunities through important organizations like HIMSS, AHIMA, and AMIA. The organizations offer their members access to employment listings, webinars, and conference events where you can network with leaders in your field while meeting potential hiring managers.

Networking Tips:

- Participate in the events that associations, including HIMSS and AMIA, organize through webinars, conferences, and local meet-ups. Connections form through networking at such events, which pave the way for beneficial professional relations and employment possibilities (Jiang et al., 2017).
- You can access professional relationships with health informatics experts and practitioners through LinkedIn. The visibility of your LinkedIn presence will grow when you create appropriate content, regularly add comments to other posts, and participate in discussions.
- Mentorship involvement will benefit your career because contacting established professionals allows them to direct

your professional journey (Jones et al., 2017; Schedlbauer et al., 2021). Mentors at your disposal complete tasks, including advice provision and job recommendation, while skill development guidance is also available.
- People in entry-level positions should make time to develop professional relationships throughout their organization besides their department. Pay attention to developing relationships between clinical personnel, information technology workers, and executive staff to establish wider organizational contacts (Masuda, 2008).

Your demonstrated professionalism and commitment through practical networking activities increase your value as an employee to potential employers (Sharp et al., 2020).

A strategic job search framework enables you to concentrate on your productivity during the entire search period. The following 30-day action guide presents an effective method to maximize your job search operations.

Job Search Checklist

- Add health informatics terminology to your resume, which suits positions in this field.
- Use LinkedIn to display your qualifications, educational credentials, and accomplishments.
- Think strategically when selecting professional associations by joining the talent pools of HIMSS, AHIMA, and AMIA.
- Submit at least five to ten applications weekly to job websites, including HIMSS, LinkedIn, and AHIMA.
- Persistent job applicants should send courteous emails to maintain their interest in employers.

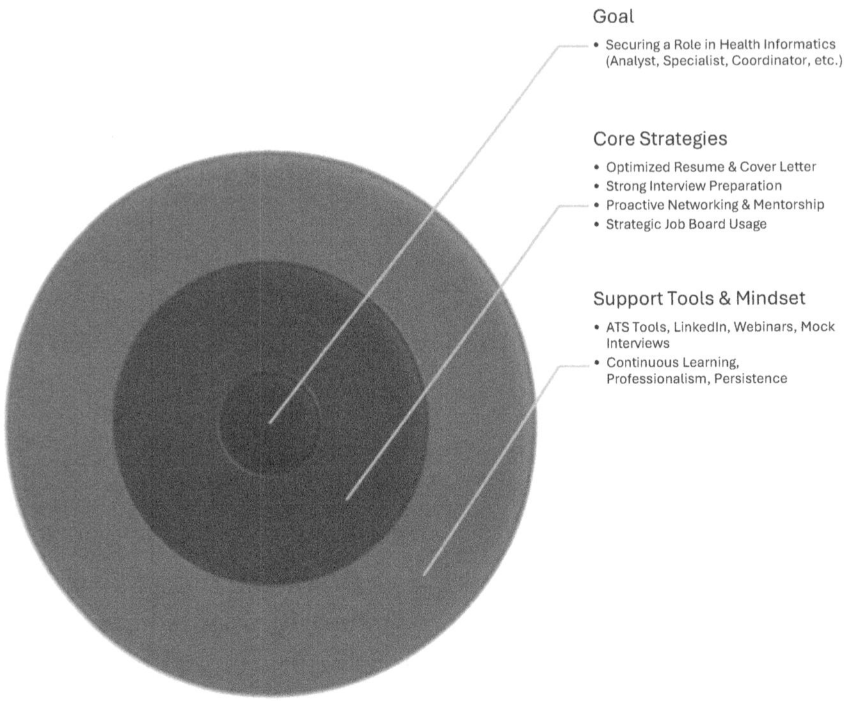

Figure 7.1 Health Informatics Job Search Ecosystem.

Figure 7.1 illustrates a job search ecosystem tailored to health informatics professionals, mapping out the synergy between personal branding, application materials, networking, and career advancement tools.

30-Day Action Plan:

- The first week requires a complete review of your resume and LinkedIn account. Make your job applications through HealthITJobs.com and AHIMA. Contact five professional individuals via LinkedIn for guidance through informal interviews.

- Your task during week 2 should include attendance at one professional association-organized meeting or one virtual webinar. You should initiate follow-ups on week 1 applications while you pursue other available job positions.
- During week 3, you should persist with job applications by choosing positions that match your qualifications and areas of interest. You should establish job alerts through LinkedIn and other platforms that post job opportunities.
- The fourth week requires follow-up communication with your professionally developed connections from networking activities. Analyze your job-hunting method along with the new information gathered from your response collection process.
- Using this strategic plan allows you to maintain job search order and engagement, which produces superior results in competitive employment situations (Bossen et al., 2019).

Summary and Reflection

Success in health informatics job searches demands professionals to unite their expertise with their abilities to interact with others. Health informatics professionals must excel at resume presentation and cover letter development while making their applications ATS-compliant and showing their technical proficiency to match market requirements for success. Candidates should dedicate their interview preparation to demonstrating their technical skills and problem-solving techniques because these traits will help them become more attractive to employers. The combination of networks through HIMSS, JobMine, AHIMA, and HealthITJobs.com job boards;

professional associations; and LinkedIn will supply you with essential career progress opportunities.

Your job search depends heavily on persistence and adaptability, which are essential to success. A planned approach toward finding new employment coupled with professional networks and updated skills creation will equip you for future changes in the health informatics sector. Your focus should remain strong while you work to enhance your brand for the rising need for skilled health informatics professionals. The right combination of employment strategies will assist you in securing a rewarding health informatics role, which builds a foundation for professional success.

Chapter 8

Professional Development and Lifelong Learning

If you pursue your career in Health Informatics, you will enjoy continuous learning because the field grows rapidly, making it an essential requirement for modern practice. The integration between technology and healthcare continues to generate the perpetual need for practitioners to continue learning about new advances and changing healthcare regulations alongside emerging technologies and evolving care practices. However, you must be on your toes to actively pursue continuous education because healthcare systems are transforming their decision-making to data-driven approaches. Professional growth in health informatics surpasses the acquisition of credentials because it requires active involvement with the broader healthcare practice community (Dalrymple, 2011).

DOI: 10.4324/9781003689843-8

The Role of Lifelong Learning in Health Informatics

Lifelong learning in health informatics encompasses various activities, from formal academic degrees to microcredentials, self-study, and professional networking (Ammenwerth & Hackl, 2015; Madlock-Brown et al., 2021). Professionals working in healthcare need to frame their perspectives toward permanent improvement and swift reactions to changing healthcare environments (Kushniruk et al., 2017). Informaticians pursuing value-based care must demonstrate complete comprehension regarding clinical workflow structures and technical integration implementation methods.

Current standards authorities and academic institutions fully support lifelong learning through their standard protocols. Amanda P. Lopez (2018) noted how the AMIA board utilizes continuing education as a fundamental competency requirement in its professional practice guidelines (AMIA, 2008). Health information technology programs today establish adaptive learning environments and competency-based education methods to create lifelong development habits in their graduates (Office of the National Coordinator for Health Information Technology [ONC], 2017). Figure 8.1 visually maps

Figure 8.1 Lifelong Learning Ecosystem in Health Informatics.

the relationship between lifelong learning methods and professional development outcomes. It illustrates how various learning resources support short-term skill acquisition and long-term career growth.

Leading Conferences for Continued Learning and Networking

The foundation of efficient lifelong learning includes active participation in professional conferences. A wide range of industrial conferences combine technical seminars with peer connection sessions that provide industry expertise and opportunities to stay in the loop about new industry developments.

HIMSS (Healthcare Information and Management Systems Society)

HIMSS is one of the world's premier events, focusing on health information and technology. The annual meeting attracts thousands of professionals who participate in cybersecurity courses and sessions about interoperability, patient engagement, and data analytical methods. Professional development at HIMSS occurs through dialogue and learning because it serves as the central gathering point for practitioners and vendors to share innovative solutions (Dalrymple, 2011).

AHIMA (American Health Information Management Association)

The conference organized by AHIMA provides the necessary education for data governance information privacy and coding and reimbursement topics, which benefits health information management professionals. AHIMA supports certification programs and offers educational activities that provide continuing education units (CEUs) to maintain credentials (AHIMA, 2024).

AMIA (American Medical Informatics Association)

AMIA organizes dual conferences that focus on serving clinical and public health and translational informatics practitioners through their Annual Symposium and Informatics Summit events. The events offer research-based content together with spaces for presentations of peer-reviewed findings. Career growth at the AMIA Learning Showcase becomes possible by unifying informatics research outputs and educational efforts with clinical practice requirements (AMIA, 2008).

HLTH (Health Innovation)

Present-day innovation-centered event HLTH connects health system leaders with startup businesses and financial investors. The HLTH event informs healthcare professionals about health sector market dynamics, technological transformation, and delivery model innovations (SHTI225, n.d.).

Scholarly Journals, Podcasts, and Blogs

People should actively follow scholarly and professional media publications to maintain informed status. Digital content and journals constitute fundamental elements of evidence-based practice development because they provide essential features for quick knowledge synthesis choices.

Recommended Journals

Health informatics features its leading journals, such as the ***Journal of the American Medical Informatics Association*** (JAMIA), ***Applied Clinical Informatics***, and ***International Journal of Medical Informatics***. Science professionals utilize these publications to offer peer-reviewed analyses of hand systems and clinical support software implementations and the processing of massive clinical datasets and health IT implementation measurements. Health informatics studies depend on these sources for both evidence-based research conclusions and academic authenticity (Kushniruk et al., 2017).

Podcasts and Blogs

Health informatics issues can be grasped efficiently through real-time information available on digital media platforms like podcasts and blogs. The digital content provided by "This Week in Health IT" and "HIMSScast" features interviews with leaders, including CIOs, medical staff, and scientists in data fields. The materials available through HealthIT.gov and Data Science Central provide readers with diagnostic AI coverage alongside information about EHR system evolutions. Consuming these media types enhances informal learning that produces meaningful results, according to Dalrymple (2011).

Continuing Education and Credentialing

The requirement for continuing education surpasses traditional academia because it sustains professional licenses, certification qualifications, and technical expertise (Klinedinst, 2022; Sapci & Sapci, 2020a). The popularity of CEUs and microcredentialing platforms rises because they provide accessible learning opportunities that help professionals achieve their aims.

Microcredentials and Online Courses

The training programs on Coursera, edX, and HIMSS Learning Center provide customizable courses that cover data science, public health informatics, cybersecurity, and interoperability. Microcredentials exist independently as qualified certifications and simultaneously support academic diploma programs. This flexible learning framework helps experts build skills without stopping their work path (Sloane et al., 2018; Dalrymple, 2011).

Institutional Support and Accreditation

Quality assurance of continuing education depends heavily on academic institutions and professional societies that ensure proper standards. Standards from CAHIIM, AMIA, and AHIMA guide curricular development and accreditation. Such guidelines enable educational programs to deliver results-based teaching methods that prepare students with current domain-specific skills (Zhang et al., 2014; Standards and Guidelines for Personal Health Records, n.d.).

Mentoring Functions as an Essential Foundation for Increasing Structural Growth

Health informatics professional growth needs mentorship as an essential aspect organizations typically overlook (El-Gayar et al., 2025; Macedo et al., 2016; Pearson & Urquhart, 2002). Health information programs deliver career mentoring and emotional assistance to establish fundamental professional growth capability beyond classroom knowledge. Skill development moves quickly when mentoring acts effectively because it trains leadership and helps professionals learn about organizational values better.

Graduate-level informatics education gets better outcomes through mentoring programs primarily because these programs enhance student confidence and bring satisfaction to their jobs and clearness to their career path (Dalrymple, 2011; AMIA, 2008). The academic-to-practice transition improves through mentorship since mentors help students understand how classroom theories translate into practical applications (SHTI225, n.d.). Training in healthcare environments enables students to understand key success factors in health IT implementation, including workflow structures, regulatory systems, and staff management principles.

The Interplay of Professional Development and Evolving Standards

The evolution of standards because of technological progress and regulatory modifications requires informatics professionals to expand their competencies (Joshi et al., 2021; Marc et al., 2019). The permanent advancement of innovation and regulatory frameworks requires healthcare professionals to plan their continuous development accordingly. Through lifelong learning, healthcare practitioners develop skillful responses to handle upcoming professional challenges.

Healthcare requires practitioners to understand genomics AI applications and digital therapeutics because of rising patient-centered care approaches and precision medicine requirements. A commitment to ongoing education regarding the most recent protocols and ethical aspects becomes mandatory for practicing medical professionals (Li et al., 2021). The ability to stay up-to-date depends on participation in specialized workshops and enrollment in brief training sessions focused on these subjects.

Designing a Personal Development Plan

Structured personal development plans enable professionals to plan their extended professional advancement. An effective personal development plan requires three elements: short-term (CEUs) and medium-term objectives that lead to new certifications and long-term aspirations focused on leadership positions. The process strongly relies on continuous evaluations for determination of growth as well as frequent self-assessments and reflections.

A personal development planner should contain these essential components that guide professional growth.

- Identify specific skills and knowledge gaps.
- Select learning resources such as journals, online courses, and mentorship opportunities that align with individual learning styles and career goals.
- A planner needs to contain realistic objectives which are specific and measurable, together with time-based deadlines.
- Professional journal logging enables students to review their educational achievements and personal development experiences.
- Achieving networking growth requires Laserton planning of both conference attendance and meeting events and professional association involvement.

Academic institutions should adopt PDPs by establishing programming that integrates with educational programs and employee performance evaluations. Personal development planning focusing on organizational aims creates team member dedication and organizational leadership quality (Sloane et al., 2018).

Summary and Reflection

One must conduct professional development and lifelong learning activities in the health informatics profession because they represent mandatory practices. Health informatics professionals must prepare for continuous growth because healthcare continues evolving exceptionally. Health informatics professionals can establish adaptable careers through involvement in major events like HIMSS and AMIA, academic learning, ongoing education programs, and mentorship experiences. Table 8.1 highlights key professional development resources and lifelong learning pathways essential for continued success in health informatics. It aligns tools, formats, and impact areas to support diverse career goals.

This chapter provides educational tools that support the professional growth of informaticians no matter what step they have in their careers. With education systems transitioning to lifelong competency-based learning models, the resources that support growth become more widely available for better impact. The health informatics field promotes employee achievement and healthcare method progress through workplace development, emphasizing continuous education.

Table 8.1 Lifelong Learning Tools and Professional Development Pathways

Development Method	*Learning Format*	*Key Platforms/ Resources*	*Career Impact*
Academic Degrees and Certificates	Formal, Structured	CAHIIM-accredited programs, Graduate Certificates	Credentialing, foundational and advanced role readiness
Conferences and Networking	Live, Interactive	HIMSS, AHIMA, AMIA, HLTH	Industry updates, connections, innovation exposure
Microcredentials and CEUs	Flexible, Online/ Hybrid	Coursera, edX, HIMSS Learning Center	Targeted skill-building, role transition support
Journals, Podcasts, and Blogs	Informal, Self-Paced	JAMIA, Applied Clinical Informatics, This Week in Health IT	Continuous awareness, EBP integration

Chapter 9

Case Studies and Real-World Applications

As we near the end of this journey, this chapter will bridge the gap between what we've already discussed and practical use. You will find some interesting case studies regarding the

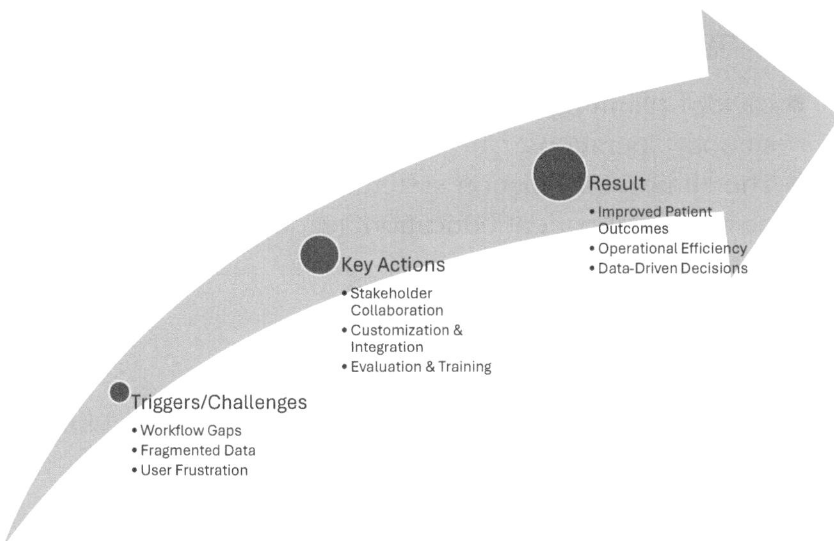

Figure 9.1 Framework for Applying Health Informatics in Practice.

DOI: 10.4324/9781003689843-9

application of health informatics. As a health practitioner, you can use these case studies as examples to excel even in your career and professional life, innovate, and use essential data and information to improve healthcare quality. Figure 9.1 visually illustrates the flow of successful health informatics case implementation, from identifying challenges to outcomes, reinforcing the importance of integrated planning, user collaboration, and iterative refinement.

Objective: Ground Theory in Experience

Case Study 1: Informatics Nurse Specialist at a Surgical Clinic (Cannon et al., 2006)

Background

A registered nurse manager overseeing surgical clinics recognized significant challenges due to inadequate informatics support during the transition to new clinical spaces and processes.

Challenges

- Lack of planning for informatics resources impeded smooth operations.
- The clinical information system lacked documentation for post-surgical patient education, leading to communication gaps.

Intervention

- The nurse manager advocated for developing and integrating appropriate documentation tools within the electronic health record (EHR) system.
- Collaborated with IT specialists to customize the EHR to include necessary educational materials.

Outcomes

- Improved documentation of patient education, enhancing continuity of care.
- Streamlined workflows within the surgical clinics, leading to increased efficiency.

Lessons Learned

- Early involvement of informatics professionals in clinical transitions is crucial.
- Customized EHR tools can significantly improve patient education and care outcomes.

Case Study 2: Data Analyst in Public Health – Indiana's Opioid Crisis (Lapowsky, 2017)

Background

Indiana faced a severe opioid crisis, marked by high prescription rates and associated health complications.

Challenges

- Disparate data sources across agencies hindered a comprehensive understanding of the crisis.
- Lack of real-time data limited timely interventions.

Intervention

- The state's Chief Data Officer led the development of an integrated opioid data center.
- Consolidated data from various agencies, including health departments, law enforcement, and social services.

Outcomes

- Enhanced ability to identify hotspots and allocate resources effectively.
- Informed policy decisions and targeted interventions to combat the opioid epidemic.

Lessons Learned

- Cross-agency data integration is vital for addressing complex public health issues.
- Real-time analytics can significantly improve response strategies.

Case Study 3: Informatics Professional at the Department of Veterans Affairs (VA) (Delio, 2003)

Background

The VA implemented the Bar Code Medication Administration (BCMA) system to reduce medication errors.

Challenges

- Nurses experienced increased workload and workflow disruptions due to the BCMA system.
- Technical issues led to frustration and workarounds that compromised the system's effectiveness.

Intervention

- Informatics professionals conducted usability assessments to identify pain points.

- Implemented system upgrades and provided comprehensive training to nursing staff.

Outcomes

- Reduction in medication errors, enhancing patient safety.
- Improved user satisfaction and system adoption among nursing staff.

Lessons Learned

- Continuous evaluation and user feedback are essential for successful health IT implementations.
- Balancing technological solutions with clinical workflows ensures better adoption and outcomes.

Summary and Reflection

The analyzed cases illustrate how health informatics is essential for changing healthcare methods across hospitals, public health, and federal systems. Table 9.1 provides a comparative summary of key real-world case studies in health informatics. Each case demonstrates how informatics-driven solutions impact clinical operations, public health, and federal healthcare systems. Through its integration, health informatics allows healthcare specialists to enhance operational processes while lowering drug delivery mistakes and execute real-time information analysis and evidence-based medical practices, resulting in better quality healthcare delivery. Health informatics projects succeed when technology is combined with appropriate advanced development work and established multidiscipline alliances in addition to sustained assessment

Table 9.1 Summary of Health Informatics Case Studies and Outcomes

Case Study	*Setting*	*Key Challenge*	*Informatics Intervention*	*Impact/ Outcome*
Informatics Nurse Specialist	Surgical Clinic	EHR lacked post-op education tools	Custom EHR documentation developed with IT	Improved patient education and clinic workflow
Data Analyst in Public Health	Indiana Opioid Crisis	Disparate data across agencies	Created integrated opioid data center	Targeted interventions and improved policy decisions
VA Informatics Professional	Veterans Affairs	Nurse dissatisfaction with BCMA system	Usability testing, system upgrades, staff training	Reduced medication errors and improved adoption

and adaptive efforts. Significant results from integrating informatics require healthcare professionals to harmonize systems with organizational cultures, technological capacities, and real clinical environments. These medical system cases demonstrate how vital user involvement and continuous system development are to preserve systems' reactions to evolving healthcare requirements. These narratives demonstrate how healthcare programs will advance through individuals who excel in uniting technological systems with healthcare personnel and compassionate patient interactions.

Chapter 10

Resources and Tools

This final chapter consolidates your journey through health informatics by equipping you with practical resources for career readiness. From professional organizations and reading lists to educational platforms and required element templates, this chapter empowers you to take actionable steps toward career success in the field.

Professional Organizations in Health Informatics

Engaging with professional organizations allows you to stay informed about industry trends, network with leaders, and access certifications and educational resources. The most influential include:

- AHIMA (American Health Information Management Association) – www.ahima.org

DOI: 10.4324/9781003689843-10

- AMIA (American Medical Informatics Association) – www.amia.org
- HIMSS (Healthcare Information and Management Systems Society) – www.himss.org
- AMCP (Academy of Managed Care Pharmacy) – www.amcp.org
- HL7 International – www.hl7.org
- ISPOR (International Society for Pharmacoeconomics and Outcomes Research) – www.ispor.org

Recommended Reading in Health Informatics

- *Health Informatics: Practical Guide* by William R. Hersh (Ed.), 8th Edition
- *Biomedical Informatics* by Edward H. Shortliffe and James J. Cimino
- *Essentials of Health Information Systems and Technology* by Jean A. Balgrosky
- *Public Health Informatics and Information Systems* by J. A. Magnuson and Brian E. Dixon (Eds.), 3rd Edition

Recommended Online Courses and Certifications

- Coursera: Specializations in Healthcare IT, Data Science, and AI for Medicine
- edX: Health Informatics MicroMasters from institutions like Georgia Tech and Doane University
- HIMSS Learning Center: Certificate programs and webinars
- AMIA 10x10 Program: Introductory and intermediate informatics education
- Udemy: Skill-building courses in SQL, Tableau, and Python for healthcare analytics

Templates for Career Success

Use the following templates as a starting point to the required elements of a professional job application package and career planning.

Cover Letter Elements – Recent Graduate

Dear [Hiring Manager's Name],
I am writing to express my interest in the Health Informatics Analyst position at [Organization Name], as advertised. With a recent degree in Health Informatics and practical experience gained through an internship, I am confident in my ability to contribute meaningfully to your team.
During my internship at [Facility Name], I supported EHR data clean-up in Epic and generated Tableau dashboards to improve care coordination. My academic capstone focused on reducing care fragmentation through health data exchange, a mission I know aligns with your organization's values.
I am eager to bring my passion for healthcare data and patient-centered care to your team. Thank you for your time and consideration. I welcome the opportunity for an interview.

Sincerely,
[Your Full Name]

Cover Letter Elements – Experienced Professional

Dear [Hiring Manager's Name],
I am excited to apply for the Senior Health Informatics Analyst position at [Organization Name].

With over seven years of experience optimizing EHR systems and leading clinical data initiatives, I offer a proven track record of transforming data into actionable insights that improve care delivery.

At [Previous Organization], I led a project to streamline provider workflows in Epic, reducing redundant documentation and saving over 400 clinician hours annually. I've also collaborated with cross-functional teams to deploy predictive analytics tools for early sepsis detection, contributing to a 15% improvement in response times.

I am enthusiastic about the chance to advance innovation at [Organization Name] and would welcome the opportunity to discuss how I can support your goals.

Best regards,
[Your Full Name]

Resume Elements – Recent Graduate

[Your Full Name]

[Your Address] | [Your City, State, ZIP] | [Your Email] | [Your Phone Number] | [LinkedIn URL]

Professional Summary

Motivated Health Informatics graduate with hands-on experience in EHR systems, data analysis, and privacy compliance. Skilled in SQL and Tableau with a strong foundation in HIPAA regulations and clinical workflows. Seeking an entry-level role to apply my training and contribute to patient-centered data initiatives.

Skills

- Electronic Health Records (EHR) | Data Analysis | HIPAA Compliance
- SQL | Tableau | Microsoft Excel
- Health IT Systems | Data Governance | Basic Python

Education

Bachelor of Science in Health Informatics
[University Name], [City, State]/[Month, Year]
GPA: 3.7 | Capstone: "Improving Access to Care Using EHR Integration"

Certifications

- Certified Associate in Health Information and Management Systems (CAHIMS)
- HIPAA Privacy and Security Training

Experience

Health Informatics Intern
[Health System or Clinic Name], [City, State] / [Month, Year] to [Month, Year]

- Maintained and updated patient charts in Epic EHR, achieving 100% documentation accuracy.
- Used Tableau to generate weekly dashboard reports for leadership.
- Supported data quality reviews across departments.

Technical Tools

Epic, Cerner (read-only), Tableau, SQL, Excel, Google Workspace

Resume Elements – Experienced Professional

[Your Full Name]

[Your Address] | [Your City, State, ZIP] | [Your Email] | [Your Phone Number] | [LinkedIn URL]

Professional Summary

Experienced Health Informatics Analyst with 7+ years in hospital and public health environments. Expert in EHR optimization, SQL-based data warehousing, privacy compliance, and cross-functional stakeholder engagement. Proven track record in translating clinical needs into data-driven solutions.

Skills

- Clinical Informatics | Data Governance | HL7 Standards
- SQL | Tableau | Python | Epic Reporting Workbench
- Change Management | Privacy Compliance | Workflow Optimization

Education

Master of Science in Health Informatics
[University Name], [City, State] / [Month, Year]
Bachelor of Science in Health Information Management
[University Name], [City, State] / [Month, Year]

Certifications

- Registered Health Information Administrator (RHIA)
- Certified Professional in Healthcare Information and Management Systems (CPHIMS)

Experience

Senior Health Informatics Analyst
[Health System Name], [City, State] / [Month, Year] to Present

- Led EHR optimization initiative reducing documentation time by 25%.
- Conducted SQL-based performance analysis, influencing policy changes for readmission reduction.
- Trained 40+ staff on best practices in clinical data entry and quality reporting.

Technical Tools

Epic, Cerner, Tableau, Python, SQL Server, SAS

Career Planning Elements – Recent Graduate

Short-Term Goals (3–6 months):

- Gain employment in a Health Informatics Analyst or EHR support role.
- Join AHIMA and attend a local HIMSS chapter event.
- Complete HIPAA and Tableau microcourses on Coursera.

Mid-Term Goals (6–18 months):

- Earn CAHIMS certification.
- Present a poster at a HIMSS or AMIA event.
- Build a professional LinkedIn network of 100+ industry contacts.

Long-Term Vision (2–5 years):

- Transition into a project management or systems analyst role.
- Begin a master's degree in Health Informatics or Public Health.

Educational Needs:

- Microcredentials in SQL, Data Visualization, Privacy Law
- CEUs via AMIA and HIMSS Learning Centers

Networking Milestones:

- Connect with two mentors in the field
- Attend at least one national conference

Skill Gap Identification:

- Improve Python fluency
- Gain hands-on experience with FHIR and HL7 standards

Career Planning Elements – Experienced Professional

Short-Term Goals (3–6 months):

- Apply to strategic leadership roles in informatics or health IT.
- Publish a white paper or LinkedIn article on a recent project.
- Join a HIMSS working group.

Mid-Term Goals (6–18 months):

- Earn CPHIMS or PMP certification.
- Serve as a panelist or workshop facilitator at AMIA or HIMSS.
- Mentor early-career professionals or interns.

Long-Term Vision (2–5 years):

- Become Chief Informatics Officer or Director of Data Strategy.

- Lead enterprise-wide digital transformation or AI integration.

Educational Needs:

- Executive education in healthcare leadership or innovation
- Advanced training in interoperability and data ethics

Networking Milestones:

- Present at national or international health informatics events
- Collaborate with interdisciplinary researchers or startups

Skill Gap Identification:

- Expand expertise in advanced analytics (e.g., machine learning)
- Deepen knowledge in regulatory tech (e.g., GDPR, 21st Century Cures Act)

Final Reflection

Your success in health informatics begins with the steps you take today. You are now equipped with both foundational knowledge and applied strategies from academic preparation to job search and career development. Leverage these tools, engage with professional communities, and commit to lifelong learning. Your journey as a health informatics leader begins now.

References

Alherz, A., Alherz, A., Alnaim, A., & Alyahya, A. (2025). Challenges and opportunities of health informatics and health information management career in Saudi Arabia: A qualitative study. *Journal of Medicine and Clinical Nursing Studies*, *3*(2), 1–8.

Alotaibi, Y. K., & Federico, F. (2017). The impact of health information technology on patient safety. *Saudi Medical Journal*, *38*(12), 1173–1180.

Alzghaibi, H. (2023). The gap between bachelor's degree graduates in health informatics and employer needs in Saudi Arabia. *BMC Medical Education*, *23*(1), 475.

American Health Information Management Association. (2024). Recertification guide: Maintenance of an AHIMA certification (Updated October 2024). AHIMA. https://www.ahima.org/media/xyvnaf24/revised-recertification-guide-7-9-25.pdf

AMIA. (2008). *AMIA 2008 Annual Symposium Proceedings*. https://www.amia.org/meetings-education

Ammenwerth, E., & Hackl, W. O. (2015). Job profiles of biomedical informatics graduates. *Methods of Information in Medicine*, *54*(04), 372–375.

Andreu-Perez, J., Poon, C. C. Y., Merrifield, R. D., Wong, S. T. C., & Yang, G.-Z. (2015). Big data for health. *IEEE Journal of Biomedical and Health Informatics*, *19*(4), 1193–1208.

Aziz, H. A. (2017). A review of the role of public health informatics in healthcare. *Journal of Taibah University Medical Sciences*, *12*(1), 78–81.

Bichel-Findlay, J., Scott, P. J., Borycki, E., Currie, L., Saranto, K., Hersh, W., Martin, G., Wainwright, D., Yogeswaran, S., Jaspers,

M., Schaper, L., Spies, C., Kuziemsky, C., Lehmann, C. U., Ronquillo, C., Nøhr, C., Valenta, A. L., Nykanen, P., Schoville, R., & Knaup-Gregori, P. (2023a). BMHI knowledge domains and educational needs. *International Journal of Medical Informatics, 170*, 104908. https://doi.org/10.1016/j.ijmedinf.2022.104908.

Bichel-Findlay, J., Koch, S., Mantas, J., Abdul, S. S., Al-Shorbaji, N., Ammenwerth, E., Baum, A., Borycki, E. M., Demiris, G., & Hasman, A. (2023b). Recommendations of the International Medical Informatics Association (IMIA) on education in biomedical and health informatics: Second revision. *International Journal of Medical Informatics, 170*, 104908.

Borycki, E. M., Foster, J., Sahama, T., Frisch, N., & Kushniruk, A. W. (2013). Developing national level informatics competencies for undergraduate nurses: Methodological approaches from Australia and Canada. *Studies in Health Technology and Informatics, 183*, 345–349.

Bossen, C., Markussen, R., & Dyb, K. (2019). Infrastructuring and ordering devices in health care: Medication plans and practices on a hospital ward. *Computer Supported Cooperative Work (CSCW), 28*(2), 209–239.

Brewer, L. C., Fortuna, K. L., Jones, C., Walker, R., Hayes, S. N., Patten, C. A., & Cooper, L. A. (2020). Back to the future: Achieving health equity through health informatics and digital health. *JMIR mHealth and uHealth, 8*(1), e14512.

Bureau of Labor Statistics (BLS). (2021). *Occupational outlook handbook: Medical and health services managers.* U.S. Department of Labor. Retrieved from https://www.bls.gov/ooh/management/medical-and-health-services-managers.htm

Cannon, M. A., Smith, K., & Bickford, C. J. (2006). Case study: A view of informatics nursing from a clinical nurse's perspective. *Studies in Health Technology and Informatics*, 122, 284–287.

Chung, W., & Zeng, D. (2017). Social-media-based policy informatics: Cyber-surveillance for homeland security and public health informatics. In *Policy analytics, modelling, and informatics: Innovative tools for solving complex social problems* (pp. 363–385). Springer.

Clarke, M. A., Moore, J. L., Steege, L. M., Koopman, R. J., Belden, J. L., Canfield, S. M., Meadows, S. E., Elliott, S. G., & Kim, M. S. (2016). Health information needs, sources, and barriers of primary care patients to achieve patient-centered care: A literature review. *Health Informatics Journal*, *22*(4), 992–1016.

Collen, M. F., & Ball, M. J. (2015). *The history of medical informatics in the United States*. Springer.

Cummins, M. R., Gundlapalli, A. V., Murray, P., Park, H.-A., & Lehmann, C. U. (2016). Nursing informatics certification worldwide: History, pathway, roles, and motivation. *Yearbook of Medical Informatics*, *25*(01), 264–271.

Dalrymple, P. W. (2011). Educating eHealth professionals: The need for continuous learning. *Medical Reference Services Quarterly*, *30*(1), 50–58.

Delio, M. (2003, January). Bar-code tech drives nurses nuts. *WIRED*. https://www.wired.com/2003/01/bar-code-tech-drives-nurses-nuts

Demiris, G. (2016). Consumer health informatics: Past, present, and future of a rapidly evolving domain. *Yearbook of Medical Informatics*, *25*(S1), S42–S47.

Dorsey, E. R., Topol, E. J., & Boulton, M. (2016). State of Telehealth. *New England Journal of Medicine*, *375*(2), 54–61.

El-Gayar, O., Wahbeh, A., Al-Ramahi, M., & Elnoshokaty, A. (2025). *Highlighting competency gaps in health informatics education using advanced text-embedding models*. In Proceedings of the 58th Hawaii International Conference on System Sciences (HICSS). https://www.researchgate.net/publication/388772017_Highlighting_Competency_Gaps_in_Health_Informatics_Education_Using_Advanced_Text_Embedding_Models

Elnoshokaty, A., Al-Ramahi, M., El-Gayar, O., Nasralah, T., & Wahbeh, A. H. S. (2023). *Mining health informatics job advertisements: Insights for higher education programs and job seekers*. In Proceedings of the 56th Hawaii International Conference on System Sciences (HICSS_56). https://aisel.aisnet.org/hicss_56/da/university_industry_collaboration/2/

Fang, R., Liu, L., Hu, P. J.-H., Wang, L., & Prybutok, V. R. (2016). Predicting adoption of electronic health records: Empirical evidence from Chinese hospitals. *Health Informatics Journal*, *22*(1), 22–39.

Fernández-Luque, L., & Bau, T. (2015). Health and social media: Perfect storm of information. *Healthcare Informatics Research*, *21*(2), 67–73.

Fitzmaurice, J. M. (2002). The state of health IT adoption and workforce in the United States. *Journal of AHIMA*, *73*(10), 58–60.

Fitzmaurice, J. M., Adams, K., & Eisenberg, J. M. (2002). Three decades of research on computer applications in health care: Medical informatics support at the agency for healthcare research and quality. *Journal of the American Medical Informatics Association*, *9*(2), 144–160.

Fitzmaurice, M., & Houghton, M. (2002). Health informatics workforce development in the United States: Challenges and opportunities. *Journal of the American Medical Informatics Association*, *9*(5), 432–438.

Fridsma, D. B. (2019). Strengthening our profession by defining clinical and health informatics practice. *Journal of the American Medical Informatics Association*, *26*(7), 585.

Fridsma, D. B., Gadd, C. S., Williamson, J. J., Steen, E. B., & Andriole, K. P. (2016). Eligibility requirements for advanced health informatics certification. *Journal of the American Medical Informatics Association*, *23*(4), 851–854.

Garde, S., Harrison, D., & Hovenga, E. (2005). Skill needs for nurses in their role as health informatics professionals: A survey in the context of global health informatics education. *International Journal of Medical Informatics*, *74*(11–12), 899–907.

Garde, S., Harrison, D., Huque, M., & Hovenga, E. J. S. (2006). Building health informatics skills for health professionals: Results from the Australian Health Informatics Skill Needs Survey. *Australian Health Review*, *30*(1), 34–45.

Gibson, C. J., Abrams, K. J., & Crook, G. F. (2015). Health information management workforce transformation: New roles, new skills and experiences in Canada. *Perspectives in Health Information Management*, *12*(Fall), 1–13.

Gray, K., & Sim, J. (2010). Factors in the development of clinical informatics competence in early career health sciences professionals. *Advances in Health Sciences Education*, *16*(1), 31–46.

Green, C. J., van Gyn, G. H., Moehr, J. R., Lau, F. Y., & Coward, P. M. (2004). Introducing a technology-enabled problem-based learning approach into a health informatics curriculum. *International Journal of Medical Informatics, 73*(2), 173–179.

Gu, D., Li, T., Wang, X., Yang, X., & Yu, Z. (2019). Visualizing the intellectual structure and evolution of electronic health and telemedicine research. *International Journal of Medical Informatics, 130*, 103947.

Gülkesen, K. H., & Haux, R. (2019). Research subjects and research trends in medical informatics. *Methods of Information in Medicine, 58*(S1), e1–e13.

Haghi, M., Thurow, K., & Stoll, R. (2017). Wearable devices in medical internet of things: Scientific research and commercially available devices. *Healthcare Informatics Research, 23*(1), 4–15.

Henry, J., Pylypchuk, Y., Searcy, T., & Patel, V. (2016). Adoption of electronic health record systems among US non-federal acute care hospitals: 2008–2015. *ONC Data Brief, 35*(35), 2008–2015.

Hersh, W. (2021). Biomedical informatics. *Biomedical Engineering Fundamentals, 31*.

Hersh, W., Hullis, K. F., Hribar, M. R., & Hsu, W. (2022). *Health informatics: Practical guide* (8th ed.). Oregon Health & Science University.

HIMSS. (2022). *2022 HIMSS healthcare cybersecurity survey.* Healthcare Information and Management Systems Society. https://www.himss.org/resources/2022-himss-healthcare-cybersecurity-survey

Holzinger, A. (2016). Interactive machine learning for health informatics: When do we need the human-in-the-loop? *Brain Informatics, 3*(2), 119–131.

Hoyt, R. E., Yoshihashi, A., & Bailey, C. (2007). *Health informatics: Practical guide for healthcare and information technology professionals* (5th ed.). Lulu Press.

Hoyt, R., Beiler, M., & Resnick, A. (2020). Clinical informatics specialists: Expanding roles, responsibilities, and skills. *Journal of the American Medical Informatics Association, 27*(5), 693–701.

Hsu, C. E., Dunn, K., Juo, H.-H., Danko, R., Johnson, D., Soto Mas, F., & Sheu, J.-J. (2012). Understanding public health informatics competencies for mid-tier public health practitioners—A web-based survey. *Health Informatics Journal, 18*(1), 66–76.

Huang, Q. R. (2007). Competencies for graduate curricula in health, medical and biomedical informatics: A framework. *Health Informatics Journal, 13*(2), 89–103.

Jiang, F., Jiang, Y., Zhi, H., Dong, Y., Li, H., Ma, S., Wang, Y., Dong, Q., Shen, H., & Wang, Y. (2017). Artificial intelligence in healthcare: Past, present, and future. *Stroke and Vascular Neurology, 2*(4), 230–243.

Joe, R. S., Otto, A., & Borycki, E. (2011). Designing an electronic medical case simulator for health professional education. *Knowledge Management & E-Learning, 3*(1), 63–71.

Jones, J. F., Zhang, E., Kulanthaivel, A., & Katta, S. (2017). What do they mean by "health informatics"? Health Information posts compared to program standards. In *MEDINFO 2017: Precision healthcare through informatics* (pp. 728–732). IOS Press.

Joshi, A., Bruce, I., Amadi, C., & Amatya, J. (2021). Developing Evidence-based Population Health Informatics curriculum: Integrating competency based model and job analysis. *Online Journal of Public Health Informatics, 13*(1), e10.

Kampov-Polevoi, J., & Hemminger, B. M. (2011). A curricula-based comparison of biomedical and health informatics programs in the USA. *Journal of the American Medical Informatics Association, 18*(2), 195–202.

Kaplan, B. (2020). Revisiting health information technology ethical, legal, and social issues and evaluation: Telehealth/telemedicine and COVID-19. *International Journal of Medical Informatics*, 143, 104239.

Kim, J. (2017). Big data, health informatics, and the future of cardiovascular medicine. *Journal of the American College of Cardiology, 69*(7), 899–902.

Kim, M. O., Coiera, E., & Magrabi, F. (2017). Problems with health information technology and their effects on care delivery and patient outcomes: A systematic review. *Journal of the American Medical Informatics Association, 24*(2), 246–250.

Klinedinst, J. (2022). Preparing the health Informatics workforce for the future. In *Nursing informatics: A health informatics, interprofessional and global perspective* (pp. 603–626). Springer.

Kohane, I. (2019). The promise and challenge of artificial intelligence in healthcare. *The Journal of the American Medical Association, 322*(5), 402–409.

Kokol, P., Saranto, K., & Vošner, H. B. (2018). eHealth and health informatics competencies: A systemic analysis of literature production based on bibliometrics. *Kybernetes, 47*(5), 1018–1030.

Kulikowski, C. A. (2022). 50 years of achievements and persistent challenges for biomedical and health informatics and John Mantas' educational and nursing informatics contributions. In *Achievements, milestones and challenges in biomedical and health informatics* (pp. 1–11).

Kushniruk, A. W., Borycki, E. M., & Kannry, J. L. (2017). Using simulation to improve the usability of health IT: Innovations from the field. *Journal of Digital Imaging, 30*(2), 303–310. https://doi.org/10.1007/s10278-016-9883-z

Lapowsky, I. (2017, September 14). Indiana, reeling from opioid crisis, arms officials with data. *WIRED*. https://www.wired.com/story/indiana-reeling-from-opioid-crisis-arms-officials-with-data/

Lee, K. H., Lee, J. H., Lee, Y., Lee, H., Lee, J. S., Jang, H. J., Lee, K. H., Han, J. H., & Jang, S. J. (2024). Impact of Health Informatics Analyst education on job role, career transition, and skill development: Survey study. *JMIR Medical Education, 10*, e54427.

Li, R., Niu, Y., Scott, S. R., Zhou, C., Lan, L., Liang, Z., & Li, J. (2021). Using electronic medical record data for research in a Healthcare Information and Management Systems Society (HIMSS) Analytics Electronic Medical Record Adoption Model (EMRAM) Stage 7 hospital in Beijing: Cross-sectional study. *JMIR Medical Informatics, 9*(8), e24405. https://doi.org/10.2196/24405

Lopez, A. P. (2018). Continuing education in health informatics: Integrating competencies for evolving professionals. *Journal of Health Informatics Education and Practice, 12*(3), 45–59.

Luo, J., Wu, M., Gopukumar, D., & Zhao, Y. (2016). Big data application in biomedical research and health care: A literature review. *Biomedical Informatics Insights, 8*, BII–S31559.

Ma, J. (2020). Health informatics education in a changing world: A review of educational models and trends. *Applied Clinical Informatics, 11*(5), 850–859.

Macedo, A. A., Ruiz, E. E. S., & Baranauskas, J. A. (2016). A survey of the job profiles of biomedical informatics graduates. *Methods of Information in Medicine, 55*(05), 473–477.

Mackert, M., Mabry-Flynn, A., Champlin, S., Donovan, E. E., & Pounders, K. (2016). Health literacy and health information technology adoption: The potential for a new digital divide. *Journal of Medical Internet Research, 18*(10), e264.

Madlock-Brown, C. R., Sharp, M. Y., & Reynolds, R. B. (2021). Assessing the prevalence of AHIMA-identified health informatics and information management careers and related skills: A cross-sectional study. *Perspectives in Health Information Management, 18*(Spring), 1k.

Mantas, J., Ammenwerth, E., Demiris, G., Hasman, A., Haux, R., Hersh, W., … & Wright, G. (2010). Recommendations of the International Medical Informatics Association (IMIA) on education in biomedical and health informatics. *Methods of Information in Medicine, 49*(2), 105–120.

Marc, D., Butler-Henderson, K., Dua, P., Lalani, K., & Fenton, S. H. (2019). Global workforce trends in health informatics & information management. In *MEDINFO 2019: Health and wellbeing e-networks for all* (pp. 1273–1277). IOS Press.

Masuda, Y. (2008). Developing competencies in clinical informatics: The role of formal education and training. *Journal of the American Medical Informatics Association, 15*(2), 161–168.

McLane, T. M., Hoyt, R., Hodge, C., Weinfurter, E., & Reardon, E. E. (2021). What industry wants: An empirical analysis of health informatics job postings. *Applied Clinical Informatics, 12*(2), 285–292.

Middleton, B., Bloomrosen, M., Dente, M. A., Hashmat, B., Koppel, R., Overhage, J. M., Payne, T. H., Rosenbloom, S. T., Weaver, C. A., Zhang, J., & Zhao, J. (2014). Health informatics and healthcare transformation: Entering the post-EMR era. *Journal of the American Medical Informatics Association, 21*(e1), e73–e79. https://doi.org/10.1136/amiajnl-2014-003337

Monkman, H., Mir, S., Borycki, E. M., Courtney, K. L., Bond, J., & Kushniruk, A. W. (2023). Updating professional competencies in health informatics: A scoping review and consultation with subject matter experts. *International Journal of Medical Informatics, 170*, 104969.

Murthy, V. K. (2022). Emerging disruptive technologies and their impact on health informatics. In *Designing intelligent healthcare systems, products, and services using disruptive technologies and health informatics* (pp. 77–94). CRC Press.

Ognjanović, I., Zoulias, E., & Mantas, J. (2024). Progress achieved, landmarks, and future concerns in biomedical and health informatics. *Healthcare, 12*(20), 2041.

Orji, R., & Moffatt, K. (2018). Persuasive technology for health and wellness: State-of-the-art and emerging trends. *Health Informatics Journal, 24*(1), 66–91.

Panayides, A. S., Amini, A., Filipovic, N. D., Sharma, A., Tsaftaris, S. A., Young, A., Foran, D., Do, N., Golemati, S., & Kurc, T. (2020). AI in medical imaging informatics: Current challenges and future directions. *IEEE Journal of Biomedical and Health Informatics, 24*(7), 1837–1857.

Patel, V. (2019). A framework for secure and decentralized sharing of medical imaging data via blockchain consensus. *Health Informatics Journal, 25*(4), 1398–1411.

Pearson, A., & Urquhart, C. (2002). Health informatics education–working across the professional boundaries. *Library Review, 51*(3–4), 200–210.

Rajamani, S., Waterfield, K. C., Austin, R., Singletary, V., Odowa, Y., Miles-Richardson, S., Winters, T., Powers, B., LaRoche, F., & Trachet, S. (2024). Training in public health informatics and technology leveraging a multi-institutional partnership model and emphasizing experiential learning. *Applied Clinical Informatics, 15*(4), 668–678.

Ravì, D., Wong, C., Deligianni, F., Berthelot, M., Andreu-Perez, J., Lo, B., & Yang, G. Z. (2017). Deep learning for health informatics. *IEEE Journal of Biomedical and Health Informatics, 21*(1), 4–21.

Rudolf, J. W., Garcia, C. A., Hanna, M. G., Williams, C. L., Balis, U. G., Pantanowitz, L., Tuthill, J. M., Gilbertson, J. R., & Pathology Informatics Alumni Group. (2018). Career paths of pathology informatics fellowship alumni. *Journal of Pathology Informatics, 9*(1), 14.

Salem, M. (2022). Blockchain applications in healthcare: A survey and analysis. *Journal of Health Information Systems, 36*(2), 110–124.

Sapci, A. H., & Sapci, H. A. (2020a). Teaching hands-on informatics skills to future health informaticians: A competency framework proposal and analysis of health care informatics curricula. *JMIR Medical Informatics*, *8*(1), e15748.

Sapci, H. A., & Sapci, A. H. (2020b). A new evaluation model for assessing e-health literacy skills: The Healthcare Informatics Skills Evaluation (HISE). *JMIR Medical Informatics*, *8*(1), e15748.

Schedlbauer, J., Raptis, G., & Ludwig, B. (2021). Medical informatics labor market analysis using web crawling, web scraping, and text mining. *International Journal of Medical Informatics*, *150*, 104453.

Sharp, T. A., McIntosh, B., & Yates, S. (2020). *Health informatics: A practical guide for healthcare and information technology professionals* (7th ed.). Lulu Press.

Sheikh, A., Anderson, M., Albala, S., Casadei, B., Franklin, B. D., Richards, M., Taylor, D., Tibble, H., & Mossialos, E. (2021). Health information technology and digital innovation for national learning health and care systems. *The Lancet Digital Health*, *3*(6), e383–e396.

Shickel, B., Tighe, P. J., Bihorac, A., & Rashidi, P. (2017). Deep EHR: A survey of recent advances in deep learning techniques for electronic health record (EHR) analysis. *IEEE Journal of Biomedical and Health Informatics*, *22*(5), 1589–1604.

SHTI225. (n.d.). *Health Informatics Learning Module SHTI225-0707*. Retrieved from uploaded file.

Slight, S., & Moore, M. (2021). The role of chief medical information officers in healthcare organizations: Leadership and professional development. *Journal of Applied Clinical Informatics*, *12*(2), 50–63.

Sloane, E., Williams, G., Thompson, F., Hall, T., & Hart, H. (2018). Best practices for development and delivery of graduate health informatics curriculum. In *Proceedings of the 24th Americas Conference on Information Systems (AMCIS 2018)*. AIS Electronic Library. https://aisel.aisnet.org/amcis2018/Workshops/Presentations/13/

Standards and Guidelines for Personal Health Records. (n.d.). *Standards Document*. Retrieved from uploaded file.

Tortorella, G. L., Fogliatto, F. S., Mac Cawley Vergara, A., Vassolo, R., & Sawhney, R. (2020). Healthcare 4.0: Trends, challenges and research directions. *Production Planning & Control*, *31*(15), 1245–1260.

Tuckson, R., Edmunds, M., & Hodgkins, M. (2017). Telehealth: A revolution in healthcare delivery. *New England Journal of Medicine*, *377*(16), 1585–1592.

U.S. Department of Health and Human Services, Office of the National Coordinator for Health Information Technology (ONC). (2017). Health IT Curriculum Resources for Educators. Retrieved from https://www.healthit.gov/topic/onc-health-it-curriculum-resources-educators

Veinot, T. C., Ancker, J. S., & Bakken, S. (2019). Health informatics and health equity: Improving our reach and impact. *Journal of the American Medical Informatics Association*, *26*(8–9), 689–695.

Veinot, T. C., Mitchell, H., & Ancker, J. S. (2018). Good intentions are not enough: How informatics interventions can worsen inequality. *Journal of the American Medical Informatics Association*, *25*(8), 1080–1088.

Wachter, R. (2016). *Making IT work: Harnessing the power of health information technology to improve care in England* (pp. 1–71). Department of Health.

Wilson, L. S., & Maeder, A. J. (2015). Recent directions in telemedicine: Review of trends in research and practice. *Healthcare Informatics Research*, *21*(4), 213–222.

Xu, J., Glicksberg, B. S., Su, C., Walker, P., Bian, J., & Wang, F. (2021). Federated learning for healthcare informatics. *Journal of Healthcare Informatics Research*, *5*, 1–19.

Zeng, X., Reynolds, R., & Sharp, M. (2009). Redefining the roles of health information management professionals in health information technology. *Perspectives in Health Information Management*, *6*(Summer), 1–8.

Zhang, C., Reichgelt, H., Rutherfoord, R. H., & Wang, A. J. A. (2014). Developing health information technology (HIT) programs and HIT curriculum: The Southern Polytechnic State University experience. *Journal of Information Systems Education*, 25(4), 295–304. https://aisel.aisnet.org/jise/vol25/iss4/4/

Index

Pages in *italics* refer to figures and pages in **bold** refer to tables.

R

S

T

For Product Safety Concerns and Information please contact our EU representative GPSR@taylorandfrancis.com Taylor & Francis Verlag GmbH, Kaufingerstraße 24, 80331 München, Germany